Wacky Laws,
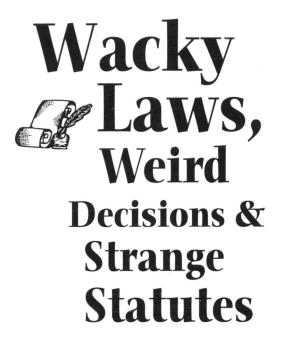
Weird
Decisions &
Strange
Statutes

Wacky Laws, Weird Decisions & Strange Statutes

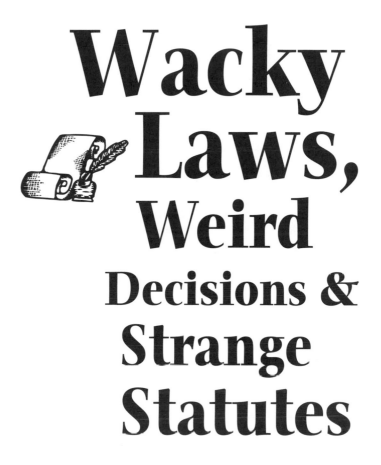

Sheryl Lindsell-Roberts, K.R. Hobbie,
Ted LeValliant & Marcel Theroux

STERLING INNOVATION
An imprint of Sterling Publishing Co., Inc.

New York / London
www.sterlingpublishing.com

STERLING and the distinctive Sterling logo are registered trademarks of
Sterling Publishing Co., Inc.

Library of Congress Cataloging-in-Publication Data Available

8   10   9   7

Published by Sterling Publishing Co., Inc.
387 Park Avenue South, New York, NY 10016
This book is comprised of material from the following Sterling titles:
Funny Laws & Other Zany Stuff © 1999 by Sheryl Lindsell-Roberts
Goofy Government Grants & Wacky Waste © 1996 by Sheryl Lindsell-Roberts
Loony Laws & Silly Statutes © 1994 by Sheryl Lindsell-Roberts
What's the Verdict? © 1991 by Ted LeValliant & Marcel Theroux
World's Wackiest Lawsuits © 1992 by K.R. Hobbie

© 2004 by Sterling Publishing Co., Inc.
Distributed in Canada by Sterling Publishing
c/o Canadian Manda Group, 165 Dufferin Street
Toronto, Ontario, Canada M6K 3H6
Distributed in the United Kingdom by GMC Distribution Services
Castle Place, 166 High Street, Lewes, East Sussex, England BN7 1XU
Distributed in Australia by Capricorn Link (Australia) Pty. Ltd.
P.O. Box 704, Windsor, NSW 2756, Australia

Designed by StarGraphics Studio

Sterling ISBN-13: 978-1-4027-1670-6
ISBN-10: 1-4027-1670-2

TABLE OF CONTENTS

I.
ON THE BOOKS:
Outlandish Statutes

Train Tribulations

In the sate of West Virginia, it's against the law to sneeze on a train.

There's a city ordinance in Andalusia, Alabama, prohibiting trains from running through the city at a speed faster than an ordinary citizen can walk.

This could be more than a free ride. There's a Connecticut law that the railroad must pay each passenger $25 if the passenger is delayed more than five minutes by a standing train.

New York Common Law: "A railway company which negligently throws a passenger from a crowded car onto the trestle is held liable for injury to a relative, who, in going to his rescue, falls through the trestle."

On the Road Again

The speed limit for ambulances is 20 mph in Port Huron, Michigan.

All fire trucks in New Orleans, Louisiana, are required to stop at red lights.

In the state of Virginia, pedestrians must beware!

If one is struck by a moving automobile, the pedestrian—not the driver—will be fined.

Every public vehicle in San Francisco, California, must be outfitted with a spittoon. That includes taxis, police cruisers, cable cars, buses, and trolleys. If the law is violated, city officials can be prosecuted.

Buenos Aires, Argentina, has a major problem with drunk drivers. Therefore, the Department of Motor Vehicles has started issuing licenses only if people can pass a drunk-driving test. The test involves driving at a high speed along a crooked, very wavy-lined highway after drinking two 12-ounce bottles of beer.

Up, Up and Away

There's a law in Maine that prohibits anyone from stepping out of a plane while it's in the air.

It's illegal for an airplane to fly over a stadium during a game in Baltimore, Maryland.

In the Eyes of the Beholder

If you want to use curlers in your hair in Oklahoma, you'd better have a curl license.

In Michigan, a woman's hair belongs to her husband.

There's an ordinance in Morrisville, Pennsylvania, that prohibits a woman from wearing cosmetics without a permit.

The Envelope, Please

California has finally answered the long-awaited question "What's the State Dirt?" As of January 1, 1998, the Official State Dirt is San Joaquin (san-wä-'ken) soil.

Amour

In Logan County, Colorado, a man isn't allowed to kiss a woman while she's asleep.

If you plan to walk down the street with another man's wife, you'd better stay away from Challis, Idaho. It's illegal.

Men in Eureka, Nevada, who have mustaches, are forbidden to kiss women.

Members of the opposite sex in Little Rock, Arkansas, can be thrown in jail for 30 days for flirting.

Before a man gets married in Truro, Mississippi, he must "prove himself worthy" by hunting and killing either six blackbirds or three crows.

And Baby Makes Three

It's against the law for children under the age of seven to go to college in Winston-Salem, North Carolina.

Although there are no R and X ratings for Ma Bell, in Blue Earth, Minnesota, it's against the law for children under 12 to talk on the telephone unless accompanied by a parent.

Kids in Kalispell, Montana, must have a note from the doctor in order to buy a lollipop or candy bar while church services are in session.

At the Paiute Indian Reservation in California, a mother-in-law is prohibited from spending more than 30 days a year visiting her kids.

Forever Hold Your Peace

Representative Linda Larason, from Oklahoma, was concerned about the divorce rate being so high. So she proposed a law stating that before a couple be issued a marriage license, they sign a contract agreeing to the following:

Neither shall snore.

At least one meal a week shall be prepared by the non-primary cook.

Toothpaste will be squeezed from the bottom of the tube and the cap shall always be put back on.

Pantyhose can't be left hanging in the shower.

And the toilet seat shall always be down when not being used.

Horsin' Around

In Waco, Texas, it's illegal to toss a banana peel on the streets because a horse could step on the peel and slip.

If you're a motorist passing through Pennsylvania

and sight a team of horses coming toward you, you must pull well off the road, cover your car with a blanket or canvas that blends in with the countryside, and let the horses pass. If one of the horses is skittish, you must take your car apart piece by piece and hide it under the nearest bush.

If you're riding through Charleston, South Carolina, your horse better be wearing diapers.

In Maysville, West Virginia, horses command the greatest respect. There's a law mandating that anyone meeting a horse and buggy on the road must bow from the waist.

It is against the law to ride down the street on an ugly horse in Wilbur, Washington.

All horses in Fort Lauderdale, Florida, must be equipped with horns and headlights.

A horse is not allowed to eat a fire hydrant in Marshalltown, Iowa.

All horses in Fountain Inn, South Carolina, are required to wear pants in public.

If you live in Omaha, Nebraska, you are required to place a hitching post in the front of your house.

In Virginia, it is illegal to permit an unhaltered horse—age one year or older—to appear in any public place of worship.

Horses cannot be turned loose in a burial ground in Vermont.

A horse in Norfolk, Virginia, may not be ridden in the waters of the Chesapeake Bay.

Vermont doesn't approve of painted ponies. If you're found painting yours, you will be arrested.

Anyone leaving horses or mules unattended (unless tied to a hitching post) will be subject to a fine in Spring Valley, New York.

If you open your umbrella in the presence of a horse in New York City, you can go to jail.

You cannot sell horse urine in Vermont unless you're licensed.

Changing the teeth of a horse to deceive another individual is illegal in Arkansas.

A horse in Connecticut must get a note from its doctor before it can be auctioned.

M-I-C-K-E-Y Mouse

Mickey Mouse is prohibited from running for public office in Comal County, Texas. The reason: "Mickey Mouse is not and has not been a resident of Comal County for six months as required by law . . . and is, therefore, under the laws of Texas, ineligible to hold office."

Holy Cow!

Men in Fruithill, Kentucky, must remove their hats when they come face to face with a cow.

This is no bull! There's a law in Leadville, Colorado, that describes how a bull must be equipped while walking on a highway. He must wear a bell, whistle or horn, headlight, and tail light.

Playing Chicken

Gainesville, Georgia, considers itself the "Chicken Capital of the World," and it's illegal there to eat chicken with a fork.

Under the Kansas Penal Code, anyone caught stealing chickens at night will be charged with grand larceny. And anyone caught stealing chickens during the day will be charged with petty larceny.

It's a Dog's Life

People who make ugly faces at dogs in Oklahoma will be fined and/or jailed.

There's an anti-necking law in New Castle, Delaware, that states: A couple may not neck—or even hold hands—while walking a dog on a leash.

'Ribbit'

If a frog's croaking keeps you awake at night in Memphis, Tennessee, you can have the frog arrested. In Hayden, Arizona, it's illegal to disturb a bullfrog.

A Nutty One

In Charleston, South Carolina, it's illegal to eat nuts on a city bus. The maximum penalty for such an infraction can be 60 days in jail and a $500 fine.

Amazing Alcohol

Men in Nyala, Nevada, are forbidden to buy drinks for more than three people in any one round.

Since 1908, Mississippi has been known as a teatotaling state. However, the state collects taxes on liquor consumed in the state. This happens on the black market, where the law says that the state can collect a 10 percent tax on "any personal property the sale of which is prohibited."

All in the Ale

You can't serve beer (or any alcoholic beverage) to a moose in Alaska.

The Encyclopedia Britannica was banned in Texas because it disclosed the formula for making beer.

It's against the law in North Dakota to serve beer with pretzels at any restaurant, bar, or club.

Missouri legislators enacted a strict law that listed all the ingredients that can be used to brew beer. Don't worry about the beer being watered down— they forgot to include water as an ingredient.

Say 'Cheese'

Apple pie in Wisconsin cannot be served without a cheese topping.

In a Pickle

In Boston, Massachusetts, legislators said a pickle should bounce four inches when dropped from waist height.

Pickles were outlawed altogether in Los Angeles, California, for fear the odor would offend people.

To be legal for sale in Connecticut, pickles must remain unbroken. They must bounce when dropped one foot above a solid oak table.

It's illegal to throw a tainted pickle into the street in Trenton, New Jersey.

In Rhode Island, it's illegal to throw pickle juice on a trolley.

Ice Cream, You Scream

It's illegal to sell ice cream after 6 p.m. in Newark, New Jersey, unless the customer has a doctor's note.

Methodist Church elders in Evanston, Illinois, were pressured to forbid the sale of ice cream sodas because they believed that "soda water" was a "mite intoxicating."

Hailing the Hack

In Annapolis, Maryland, it's against the law for a cab driver to lock female passengers in their taxis. The law can impose a $500 fine and three years' probation.

Cab drivers must be careful whom they pick up in Magnolia, Arkansas. A local ordinance mandates that "Cab drivers may not knowingly carry a person of questionable or bad character to his or her destination."

Firefighting

In St. Louis, Missouri, it's illegal for an on-duty fireman to rescue a woman wearing a nightgown. If the woman wants to be rescued, she must be fully clothed.

The Lap of Luxury

A secretary can't be alone in a room with her boss in Pasadena, California.

Never on Sunday

Dominos players should be careful about playing the game in Alabama on Sundays. It's illegal.

A merchant can sell custom-made drapery on Sunday in Morristown, New Jersey, but he can't sell the hardware to hang the drapery until Monday.

In Nashville, Tennessee, police began enforcing the Sunday closing laws and many people were arrested. Judge Andrew Doyle claimed that on Sunday people could only do acts of charity. He ordered arrests for buses that were running, shows that were open, and preachers who were preaching.

"We are going to close this town down," Judge Doyle exclaimed.

Restaurant owners beware. It's illegal to sell Limburger cheese on Sunday if you live in Houston, Texas, or to sell cherry pie à la mode if you live in Kansas.

Drugstores in Providence, Rhode Island, may sell toothbrushes on Sunday, but not toothpaste.

And in Columbus, Ohio, you cannot legally sell corn flakes on Sunday.

"Never on Sunday" is what a Hartford, Connecticut law says about kissing your wife.

The sale of ice cream was banned on Sundays in Ohio, because it was deemed frivolous and luxurious. Merchants, therefore, began topping the ice cream with scoops of fruit thereby deeming the dish healthy and nutritious. Lo and behold, the "ice cream sundae" was invented.

In Ohio, "sporting, rioting, quarreling, hunting, and shooting" were deemed illegal on Sundays.

Let the Truth Prevail

Campaigners in Waterbury, Vermont, are prohibited from "telling lies or fabricating stories" while on the campaign trail.

State of Confusion

When the state of Oklahoma was first organized, legislators spent 88 out of the first 90 days arguing over the location of the capital. During the two remaining days, frivolous laws were passed. One empowered the territory to license sea pilots. Another prohibited anyone from fishing for whales off the coast.

Political Potpourri

In Maryland, two legislators, ironically named Masters and Johnson, recently introduced a bill to create a board to license sex therapists.

Voters in McCook, Nebraska, aren't allowed to show up at the polls on roller skates. And in Texas no one's allowed to carry a spear or sword to the polls.

Politicians in both Oxford and Cleveland, Ohio, passed rules making it a violation for women to wear patent leather shoes.

Food for Thought

In Sugartown, Louisiana, politicians must refrain from squirting tobacco juice on the sidewalk while on the campaign trail.

Politicians in Preston, Idaho, aren't allowed to eat onions before speaking before a large group of voters within the city limits.

Voters in Crookston, Minnesota, are banned from nibbling on popcorn while listening to a political speech.

No one in Sydney, Ohio, is allowed to carry a "sack of Spanish peanuts" to a political rally or chew the peanuts while the candidate is speaking.

Dress for Success

All politicians in Fairfield, Illinois, must wear shirts with buttons running up the front when they're running for public office.

All campaigners must wear long pants when walking down the streets or shaking hands with prospective voters in San Angelo, Texas.

Any woman in Wheatfield, Indiana, who's wearing shorts, a halter top, or bathing suit to a political rally can be found guilty of a misdemeanor.

And any adult who strolls around barefoot at a political rally in Elizabethtown, Kentucky, had better beware!

All in the Game

A local ordinance in Atwoodville, Connecticut, prohibits people from playing Scrabble while waiting for a politician to start speaking.

Candidates in Clewiston, Florida, aren't allowed to play chess to pass the time.

Splish-Splash

There's a law in Lander, Wyoming that prohibits people from taking a bath when the cold weather sets in. However, adults are allowed to bathe once a month, children not at all.

Morristown, Vermont, prohibits people from taking baths unless they've gotten permission from the Board of Selectmen.

In the state of Wisconsin, there's a law stating that "Every proprietor of a lumber camp must supply an individual bathtub for each lumberjack in his employ."

It's illegal in Virginia to take a bath in a tub if the tub is located in any room attached to the house.

All bathtubs installed in the state of Maine must have four legs. If it doesn't have any legs, it must be installed outside the home.

A Florida law requires one to wear clothing when taking a bath.

A woman cannot take a bath in a business office in Carmel, California.

Falling asleep in a bathtub in Detroit, Michigan, is illegal.

Everyone must take a bath on Saturday night in Barre, Vermont.

Having a bathtub in your house in the state of Virginia is forbidden. It must be kept in the yard.

If you live in Minneapolis, Minnesota, and plan to install a bathtub, be certain that it has legs.

Residents in Berkley, California, are required to fill bathtubs and unplug them simultaneously. (This was to drown rats in the sewer system.)

Taking a bath during the winter months is against the law in Indiana.

Those in the state of Virginia who own bathtubs must pay a $30 levy for each.

In Brooklyn, New York, it is illegal for a donkey to sleep in a bathtub.

What Would Henry Ford Say?

You cannot drive a car in Tennessee while you are asleep.

You cannot operate any motor vehicle while sitting in someone's lap in Cleveland, Ohio.

It is illegal in Macomb, Illinois for an auto to impersonate a wolf.

Blind men are forbidden to drive automobiles in New York.

A motorist in Milwaukee cannot park an auto for more than two hours unless hitched to a horse.

A woman in California is forbidden to drive a car in a housecoat—and in Alabama you cannot drive a car while barefoot or in bedroom slippers.

Anyone who double-parks an auto in Minneapolis shall be put on a chain gang and fed bread and water.

Your car is forbidden to backfire in Rutland, Vermont.

A car in Glendale, Arizona, is not allowed to back up.

In Youngstown, Ohio, it is against the law to run out of gas.

Each driver on a country road in Omaha, Nebraska is required to send up a skyrocket every

150 yards, wait eight minutes for the road to clear, and then drive cautiously, blowing the horn while shooting off Roman candles.

While driving in Massachusetts, it's illegal to shave your whiskers.

It is illegal to drive an auto in Decatur, Illinois, without a steering gear.

When an auto approaches the city limits of Emporia, Kansas, a passenger from said auto must precede the auto on foot and warn people that it is approaching so that all horses can get out of the street.

Driving your auto in any downtown district was deemed illegal in Ohio.

You'd better not get caught wiping your car in San Francisco with used underwear. It's unlawful.

A woman cannot drive a car in Memphis, Tennessee, unless a man is running or walking in front of the car waving a red flag to warn approaching pedestrians and motorists.

In Transit

It is illegal in the state of Florida to transport livestock aboard school buses.

Bullfrogs cannot be exported out of Arkansas.

Transporting a stolen hemlock, cedar, or spruce is illegal on a public highway in Vermont.

Moving Right Along

Unless you have permission or it is a true emergency, jumping from a plane or dropping an object from a plane is illegal in Vermont.

An ordinance in Brewton, Alabama, specifically requires all people on city streets to either walk or ride. They cannot crawl, sleep, or stand.

A person in Johnson City, New York, is not allowed to wander from the left side of the sidewalk to the right.

It is illegal in San Francisco to discard a boat or an ark on any submerged street.

In Youngstown, Ohio, it's illegal to ride on the roof of a taxi.

All taxis must carry brooms and shovels in Washington, D.C.

A cabbie in Albuquerque, New Mexico, is forbidden to reach out and pull prospective passengers into the cab.

And it's against the law in Maine to walk down the street with your shoelaces untied.

An ordinance in Atlanta, Georgia, forbids "smelly people" to ride public streetcars.

Anyone riding a tricycle on the sidewalk in Spring Valley, New York, will be subject to a fine.

Boarding a plane in Canada while it's in flight is illegal.

It is illegal to cross the street on Sunday, in Marblehead, Massachusetts, unless it is absolutely necessary.

Airplanes are forbidden to fly over Thomasville, North Carolina, on Sundays during the hours of 11 a.m. and 1 p.m.

Disorderly Conduct

In Florida, anyone found underneath the sidewalks will be found guilty of disorderly conduct.

You're Right on Track

The legislature in the state of Kansas passed a law stating: "When two trains approach each other at a crossing, both shall come to a full stop and neither shall start up again until the other has gone."

A conductor in Illinois, must wear "his" hat while collecting fares.

A traffic law in the state of New York states: "Two vehicles that are passing each other in opposite directions shall have the right of way."

You risk going to jail in Minnesota if you are found standing in front of a moving train.

No railroad train may roll through Gainesville, Florida, faster than a man can walk.

It's a crime punishable by death to put salt on a railroad track in Alabama.

Lights Out

The Board of Supervisors in San Diego County, California, recently enacted a statute that requires all commercial lighting in the unincorporated parts of the county to be turned off at 11:00 pm. The reason: The light pollution was affecting the performance and results of the astronomers at the world-famous

Mount Palomar telescope. To show their appreciation, the scientists named an asteroid for San Diego.

Just Kid-ding

Stubborn children are considered vagrants in Jupiter Inlet Colony, Florida.

Thank goodness Ringo, John, George, and Paul were from Liverpool, because it's against the law in Mesquite, Texas, for youngsters to have unusual haircuts.

A parent in Indiana cannot drink beer if a child is in the same room.

It's illegal to pretend that your parents are rich in the state of Washington.

In Lynn, Massachusetts, babies may not be given coffee.

It's illegal in the state of Washington, to sell comics to minors if the comics might incite them to violent or immoral acts.

Kids in Fort Wayne, Indiana, can't sell their parents' jewelry.

Massachusetts passed a law in 1648 deeming that if a man has a stubborn or rebellious son who disobeys his father and/or mother, said son shall be put to death. (This law has since been repealed by the legislature.)

In Roderfield, West Virginia, only babies are allowed to ride in baby carriages.

If you live in the state of Louisiana, you can grow as tall as you want.

It is illegal in Vermont to allow your sheep to run wild in a schoolyard.

The Family
That Prays Together . . .

Ministers in Pennsylvania cannot perform a marriage ceremony if the bride or groom is drunk.

In Vermont, you could be fined up to $200 if you denied the existence of God.

It's illegal to use a reptile during any part of a religious service in Kentucky.

It's against the law in Key West, Florida, to spit on the floor of a church.

The state of Massachusetts forbids the eating of peanuts in church.

Spokane, Washington, had a law making it illegal for a race horse to interrupt a religious meeting.

And racing horses is banned on Good Friday and Easter Sunday in Delaware.

In 1659, Massachusetts outlawed Christmas. The law stated that "anybody found observing Christmas in any way" would be fined five shillings.

A member of the city council introduced a bill in Albuquerque, New Mexico, banning Santa Claus.

House Rules

A housewife in California can go to jail if she does not cook her dustcloth after using it.

In Jackson, Mississippi, if you want to set fire to your house, you must first remove the top.

There was an ordinance in Belhaven, North Carolina, permitting a sewer service charge of "$2 per month, per stool." That has recently been revised to read "per toilet."

A tenant is forbidden to bite his/her landlord if living in Rumford, Maine.

Don't Touch Me

You could go to jail in Georgia if you slap an old pal on the back.

Food Junkies

In New Jersey, it is against the law to slurp soup.

It is illegal to shoot open a can of food in Indiana.

The mixing of cornmeal or any other flour with wheat flour is illegal in Maryland.

The maximum degree of insect infestation and mold that may be permitted in cocoa beans is six percent. (In reality, this is allowed only because it is impossible for anything that is grown to avoid contact with air and earth.)

In Los Angeles, California, customers in meat markets are forbidden to poke turkeys to see if they are tender.

Ostrich steaks are exempt from state sales tax in California.

You are forbidden to offer anyone a glass of water

in Walden, New York, unless you have been issued a permit.

You need a cheesemaker's license to make cheese in Wisconsin. But to make Limburger cheese, you must have a master cheesemaker's license.

A law in Waterloo, Nebraska, prohibited barbers from eating garlic.

In the state of Tennessee, it's illegal to throw a banana peel on the sidewalk.

It's against the law to steal crawfish in Louisiana.

In Hammond, Indiana, it is illegal to throw watermelon seeds on the sidewalk.

Amusing Yourself

One cannot attend the theater in Gary, Indiana, within four hours of eating garlic.

It is illegal in Wyoming to obstruct the view of "fellow" spectators by wearing a hat in any public theater or place of amusement. (You could have to shell out $10 for this offense.)

Wearing a bonnet in a public place of amusement is also not allowed in Montana.

And in Gary, Indiana, a fine could be imposed on any theater owner who permitted patrons to wear their hats and/or bonnets in the establishment.

Also in Gary a fine of $200 could be imposed upon a child performing as a singer, musician, or gymnast. (This was repealed in 1953.)

A person in Ohio exhibiting a puppet show, wire

dancing, or tumbling could be fined $10 for engaging in "immoral practice."

It's against the law in New York to do anything that's against the law.

Is Anybody Inn?

In Boston, Massachusetts, a man entered a very posh hotel and requested a room. The desk clerk refused to assign him a room on the grounds that the man was improperly attired for such a swanky hotel. Without saying a word the "prospective guest" made his exit. He quickly changed his clothes—donning his best attire, which might have gained him access to Buckingham Palace. He also gathered sheep, cattle, and all the livestock he could locate and he and his animals entered the lobby of the hotel. The desk clerk was absolutely aghast! But he had to give the man and all his livestock rooms. Why? There is a law in existence in the Boston area, that any hotel or inn must make rooms available for a man and his livestock.

If you are staying in California, do not peel an orange in your hotel room; it's illegal.

It's illegal to register in a hotel under an assumed name in New Hampshire.

Have You Ever Heard of the 'Nine-Foot Sheet Law?'

In Oklahoma there was a legendary legislator named Alfalfa Bill Murray. He was a rather tall chap and was continually irked when he went into hotels and found the bed linens too short to cover his long, lanky body. So in 1908 he had a law passed requiring all hotels to have nine-foot sheets.

Pigging Out

Public eateries in Bristow, Oklahoma, are required to serve each patron a peanut with a shell for every glass of water served.

If you are dining at a restaurant, boarding house, club, or hotel in Wisconsin, the management is required to serve you—at no charge—$^2/_3$ ounce of their famous cheese, provided you purchase a meal that costs at least 25 cents.

In Marion, Ohio, cream puffs were once declared against the pure food and drug laws.

It is prohibited for a waiter to serve wine in a tea cup in Topeka, Kansas.

Margarine in Vermont cannot be served in a public eating place unless a notice is displayed that it is being offered.

It is illegal to eat in a place that is on fire in Chicago.

Eateries in Kansas are not allowed to serve ice cream on cherry pie.

In Omaha, Nebraska, two people are forbidden to use the same finger bowl.

It is forbidden to eat rattlesnake meat in public in Kansas.

Nebraska tavern owners may not sell beer unless they are simultaneously brewing a kettle of soup.

In Manzanita, Washington, a bartender can be fined for listening in on conversations between patrons.

Xenia, Ohio, has made it illegal to spit in a salad bar.

The Dating Game

If you are sending a box of candy to your sweetheart in Idaho, it must weigh a minimum of 50 pounds.

In Dyersburg, Tennessee, it is illegal for a girl to telephone a guy asking for a date.

A man could be fined $100 or more in Ohio if he represents himself as unmarried and keeps company with a "female of good character."

Men in North Carolina: It's illegal to talk to a woman attending an all-women's college while she's on campus.

And women: Never, never propose marriage to a man if you live in or are passing through Whitesville, Delaware. You can be nailed for "disorderly conduct."

In Portland, Maine, tickling a girl under the chin with a feather duster is illegal.

Kissing' Cousins

Kissing on the lips in Riverside, California, is in violation of a local health ordinance, unless both parties first wipe their lips with carbonized rose water.

A kiss in Halethorpe, Maryland, cannot last longer than a second.

Kissing a stranger in Cedar Rapids, Iowa is illegal.

Any man who constantly kisses "human beings" is forbidden to have a moustache if he lives in Indiana.

Sorry, My Dance Card Is Full

In Compton, California, cheek-to-cheek dancing is prohibited.

Nothing shady—but in Monroe, Utah, daylight must be visible between couples on a dance floor.

Wiggling on the dance floor is illegal in Stockton, California.

If a woman is in Bellingham, Washington, she is forbidden to take more than three steps backwards while dancing.

Iowa City and Belt, Montana, have variously banned: the grizzly bear, the bunny hug, the Texas tommy, the turkey trot, the tango, the duck wobble, the angle worm wiggle and the kangaroo glide.

A mayor in Boston once banned midnight dancing within the city limits.

Girls: In Norfolk, Virginia, you'd better not go to a public dance unless you're wearing corsets. That's the law!

The New York State Assembly passed a law outlawing the tango, the rumba, the mambo, and the cha cha.

Infants in Los Angeles cannot dance in public halls.

Dancing in Public Places in Minnesota

It's not allowed. Lighting must be very bright.
You must obtain a permit before holding a dance.
No one is permitted to perform any indecent or immoral dances.
Rude or indecent speech isn't allowed either.

Till Death Do Us Part

If a lady in Dixie, Idaho, berates her husband in public and a crowd gathers, the husband is subject to a fine.

It is illegal to remarry the same man four times in Kentucky.

A man in Tennessee is forbidden to divorce his wife unless he leaves her ten pounds of dried beans, five pounds of dried apples, a side of meat and ample yarn to knit herself stockings for a year.

A marriage in Delaware may be annulled if entered into on a dare.

In Michigan, a man owns his wife's clothes. Therefore, if she leaves him, he can follow her into the street and remove them!

A husband cannot kick his wife out of bed in Lebanon, Tennessee, even if her feet are cold; however, a wife can kick her husband out of bed without provocation.

First cousins in West Virginia may marry unless the female is 55 years old.

A man can curse and/or abuse his wife in Virginia provided he does it in a low voice.

In Pennsylvania, a man cannot be accused of desertion if his wife rents his room to a boarder and crowds him out of the house.

Dunlap, West Virginia, has rendered it illegal to tear up a marriage certificate.

You will be in violation of the law in Chillicothe, Missouri, if you throw rice at the bride and groom.

In Colorado, you will be in violation of the law if you throw shoes at the bride and groom.

Just Between Us Girls

It's illegal In Los Angeles, California, to hang your lingerie in public view.

A Florida law forbids a housewife from breaking more than three dishes a day.

If you're a woman of "notorious bad character," it's illegal to ride a horse through town.

In Gloversville, New York, women wrestlers are forbidden to appear in the city.

If you're a young woman in Corvallis, Oregon, you are forbidden to drink coffee after six in the evening.

In Kentucky: No female shall appear in a bathing suit on any highway unless she is escorted by at least two officers or is armed with a club.

The amendment reads: "The provisions of this statute shall not apply to females weighing less than 90 pounds nor exceeding 200 pounds, nor shall it apply to female horses."

How Old Are You Now?

In Wisconsin: If you are over 21, you are not required to divulge your age. Instead you can use the following code.

A = 20's
B = 30's
C = 40's
D = none of the above

For Men Only

There's a law in Brainerd, Minnesota, requiring every male to grow a beard.

In Illinois, a law requires all healthy males between the ages of 21 and 50 to work in the streets two days per year.

There may be no such thing as a bald man—just one who has grown too tall for his body; however, in New York City men are breaking the law if they enter beauty shops to have their hair regrown.

Watch for the Droppings

It is against the law in California to detain a homing pigeon.

Birds have the right of way on public highways in Utah.

A person cannot intentionally kill a bird in Vermont from an aircraft.

It is illegal in Oklahoma to rob a bird's nest from a public cemetery.

Because buzzards are classified as "songbirds" in Ohio, it is illegal to sell or buy them.

In Bayonne, New Jersey, it is against the law for a pigeon to fly overhead without a license.

Birds Not Safe in Michigan

Citizens of Michigan may receive two cents for every English sparrow they kill during the months of December, January, and February. (In order to collect, the bird's well-preserved body must be presented to the village or town clerk.)

Crows or starlings are not safe either. Each starling is worth three cents. Each crow is worth ten cents. (You must present at least 50 well-preserved starlings or 10 or more crows.) Killing the wrong bird in any of these cases is a misdemeanor.

Shh . . . Shh . . .

It's unlawful in Berkley, California, to whistle for an escaped bird before seven in the morning.

You can't honk a horn in San Antonio, Texas.

It's against the law to play the piccolo in Tryon, North Carolina, between the hours of 11 p.m. and 7:30 a.m.

If Not for Noah . . .

Don't bother trying to secure a giraffe to a telephone pole or street lamp in Atlanta; it is against the law.

In Seattle, Washington, it is unlawful for goldfish to ride a city bus in a bowl unless they are kept still.

You are not allowed to have a hippopotamus in your possession in Los Angeles.

In Youngstown, Ohio, you cannot keep a bear without a license.

If you want to carry a bear down a highway in Missouri, it must be caged; otherwise you are breaking the law.

While in Virginia, it is against the law to drive an unconfined bear down the street.

It is against the law in Alaska to disturb a grizzly bear for the purpose of taking its picture.

Camels are not allowed to wander the streets unattended in Galveston, Texas.

Buffalo cannot be driven through the streets in Newton, Kansas.

In Arkansas, it is illegal to blindfold cows on public highways.

Hens in Norfolk, Virginia, cannot lay eggs before 8 am or after 4 pm.

It is illegal in Arizona to shoot or hunt camels.

Be kind to your oysters in Baltimore, Maryland. It is forbidden to mistreat them.

In Washington, D.C. it is illegal to punch a bull in the nose.

You cannot milk anybody else's cow but your own in Texas.

Be prepared to pay $2 per bird if you sell live fowl tied by the legs in Baltimore, Maryland.

Any animal that is out after dark in Berea, Ohio, must display a tail light.

It's illegal in North Carolina to take a deer swimming in water above its knees.

Don't molest an alligator in Miami; it's against the law.

Chicken thieves in Kansas are not allowed to work during daylight hours.

It's taboo to walk your pet alligator down Main Street in Charleston, South Carolina.

If your billy goat is running loose in Wisconsin, you'd better be prepared to pay $5 to the person who finds it.

You can be fined if your swine runs in a public park in Vermont without the permission of a selectman.

If you are in McDonald, Ohio, you cannot march your goose down the main street.

In Quitman, Georgia, it's illegal for a chicken to cross the road.

Reel Estate

If you are going to a cemetery in Muncie, Indiana, you must leave your fishing tackle at home.

Fishing with explosives in Ohio is against the law.

It is illegal to fish on horseback in the District of Columbia.

You cannot fish with your bare hands in Kansas.

On the Chicago breakwater, it is illegal to fish in pajamas.

Fish cannot be transported into New York State via parcel post.

Goldfish cannot be used as bait.

Frogs may be taken from their ponds in New York from June 16 to September 30 provided it is between sunrise and sunset.

Any overt physical action intended to frighten fish is prohibited in New York State.

Anyone younger than 16 or older than 70 can fish without a license.

Dynamite cannot be used to catch fish in Illinois.

It's a criminal offense in Oklahoma to give liquor to a fish.

Never shoot a fish with a bow and arrow in Louisville, Kentucky.

And don't shoot pickerel or northern pike with a gun in Vermont's Lake Champlain.

In the state of Washington, you can't catch a fish by throwing a rock at it.

Also in the state of Washington, you are in violation of the law if you molest a food fish.

There is a "Human-Dolphin Shared Environment" law that was enacted to improve the relationship between humans and "local resident" marine life.

Until recently it was illegal to fish for whales off the coast of Oklahoma.

Hee-Haw!

Unless your mule is wearing a straw hat, it is against the law in Lang, Kansas to drive down Main Street.

It is necessary to document any services performed by a jackass in Baltimore.

In Ohio, it is against the law to set a fire under your mule if it balks.

If your two-year-old mule runs wild in Arkansas and is not claimed within two days, anyone may castrate the animal. (Once this action has been performed, it will cost you a three dollar service charge.)

A Hare-Raising Experience

One is forbidden to shoot rabbits in New York City from the back end of a Third Avenue streetcar when it is in motion.

You can't shoot rabbits from a motorboat in Kansas.

It is against the law in Statesville, North Carolina, to race rabbits in the street.

More than eight rabbits are not allowed to reside on the same block in Tuscumbia, Alabama.

It's a Dog's Life

You cannot take a French poodle to the opera in Chicago.

People are not allowed to participate in dog fights in Idaho.

Your dog cannot get an education in Hartford, Connecticut.

A police officer in Pauling, Ohio, may bite a dog in an attempt to quiet him.

All dogs must pay full fare and cannot transfer on the tramways in Denver.

An ordinance in Belvedere, California, states: "No dog shall be in a public place without its master on a leash."

Dogcatchers in Houston, Texas, must submit to psychoanalysis to determine their eligibility to chase stray mutts.

Denver passed a law in 1936 stating that a dogcatcher must notify dogs of impounding by posting a notice for three consecutive days on a tree in the city park and along a public road running through the park.

There's a law in Chicago that forbids anyone from feeding whiskey to dogs.

If a bitch is found running about Joliet, Illinois, the owner is liable for a $1 to $10 fine.

The Tower of Babble

Speaking English in the state of Illinois is illegal. In 1919, author H.L. Mencken had a statute revised establishing "American" as the official language.

Fighting Like Cats and Dogs

Cats and dogs are not allowed to fight in Barber, North Carolina.

In International Falls, Minnesota, cats are forbidden to chase dogs up telephone poles. (That also refers to pole cats.)

A pet in Sterling, Colorado, cannot run loose without a tail light.

An Eye for an Eye

Should your dentist in South Foster, Rhode Island, make the mistake of pulling the wrong tooth, he can be penalized by being required to appear at the village blacksmith to have the corresponding tooth removed from his mouth.

Dress Code

If you are in Nevada, you'd better not have a hatpin stick out beyond your hat more than a half-inch.

Street vendors in Zion, Illinois, are required to wear shirts, blouses, and shoes.

If you plan to go swimming in Rochester, Michigan, you must first have your bathing suit inspected by the police.

Everyone walking on the street in Elko, Nevada, is required to wear a mask.

It is illegal in Atlanta to dress a mannequin unless the shades are pulled down during the robing and disrobing period.

They "let it all hang out" in Nogales, Arizona. It is illegal to wear suspenders.

A 200-pound woman in Gurnee, Illinois, may not ride a horse in shorts.

Getting to Work

In Altoona, Pennsylvania, it is illegal for a babysitter to clean out the employer's refrigerator.

The milkman cannot run while making deliveries in St. Louis, Missouri.

Roller skating instructors in Indiana are forbidden to lead their students "astray" during lessons.

It is illegal in Wyoming to eliminate cuspidors for the use of employees.

Even if your boss is a stinker, in Michigan, it is against the law to put a skunk in his desk.

Uncle Ben's Barber Shoppe

No one can fall asleep in a barber shop while having his hair cut in Erie, Pennsylvania.

Sleeping in a barber shop all night in Alabama is not allowed.

The state house of representatives in Baton Rouge, Louisiana, passed a law stating that a maximum of 25 cents can be charged to cut the hair off bald men.

It is illegal in Omaha, Nebraska, to shave a man's chest.

A barber in Elkhart, Indiana, cannot threaten to cut off the ears of kids.

Barbers are forbidden in Waterloo, Nebraska, to eat onions between the hours of 7 a.m. and 7 p.m.

A woman in Lindenhurst, New York, is not allowed to give a man a permanent wave.

Barbers in Milwaukee, Wisconsin, cannot use powder puffs to practice their trade.

Shop Till You Drop

It's illegal to sell suntan oil after noon on Sunday in Provincetown, Massachusetts.

If you happen to be on a shopping spree in Joliet, Illinois—beware. It's illegal for you to try on more than six dresses in any one store.

It's also illegal to mispronounce the name "Joliet."

You may not buy a hat in Owensboro, Kentucky, unless your husband has first had the opportunity to try it on.

There's a law in Magnolia, Arkansas, that regulates the sale of green meat.

Can't a Person
Get Any Sleep Around Here?

In Dunn, North Carolina, there is a law outlawing snoring and disturbing one's neighbors. The police can impose a 2- or 3-day jail sentence.

You may not sleep in a refrigerator if you are in Pittsburgh, Pennsylvania.

It's illegal in Florida to doze off under a hair dryer.

That's Killing Me!

If you live and/or work in Natoma, Kansas, it is in violation of the law to throw a knife at anyone wearing a striped suit.

You are legally permitted to hunt with a rifle in Norfolk County, Virginia, provided you are at least 50 feet off the ground.

In Frankfort, Kentucky, one is forbidden to shoot off a policeman's tie.

If a man accused of a felony in North Dakota refuses to accompany you to the police station, you are legally entitled to shoot him.

South Carolina considers it a capital offense to inadvertently kill someone while attempting suicide.

Anyone in Montana who slays or disables another in a duel must support the victim's family.

Rats

Kill any of the following in Michigan and you receive ten cents: black rats, brown rats, grey rats, Norway rats, house rats, barn rats, and wharf rats. (In order to collect, their well-preserved heads must be given to the village or town clerk and you must deliver not fewer than five at a time.)

It's a Beautiful World

If you're ugly or grotesque and live in San Francisco, you'd better stay off the streets during certain times of the day.

Go Directly to Jail
and Don't Collect $200

A prisoner in Charleston, South Carolina, can be charged $1.00 for the ride.

It is against the law in White Cloud, Kansas, to break out of jail.

In Kulpmont, Pennsylvania, it is against the law to keep a prisoner incarcerated on Sundays.

The state of Illinois permits the imprisonment of animals.

No Ifs, Ands, or Butts

No person is allowed to chew tobacco without an M.D.'s permission in Connecticut.

It is illegal to smoke a pipe after sunset in Newport, Rhode Island.

While fishing in Berkley, California, it is illegal to smoke.

What a Dead Beat

It is a misdemeanor in New York to arrest a dead man for being in debt.

Funeral directors in Nevada can be arrested for using profane or obscene language in the presence of a dead person.

Until as recently as 1975 it was illegal for a police officer in Maine to arrest a body.

Rogues & Vagabonds

Persons in Maryland can be deemed rogues or vagabonds and sent to jail if:
- they are carrying a picklock, key, jack, bit, or crow in a dwelling house, storehouse, stable, motor vehicle, or outhouse.
- they are carrying a pistol, hanger, cutlass, or bludgeon.

Persons who are not insane are guilty of a misdemeanor in Maryland if they wander about the state and lodge in a marketplace, barn, barrack, outhouse, or the open air.

It's an Act of Treason

It is considered treason to wage war against Indiana while living there.

Fire! Fire!

"Practice may make perfect," and in Fort Madison, Iowa, there is a law requiring firemen to practice for 15 minutes before attending a fire.

Firemen must wear ties while on duty in Rochester, New York.

Only the first four firemen who show up at a fire in Zeigler, Illinois, will receive financial remuneration for their services.

When School's Out

It is illegal to fly a kite in the District of Columbia.

No person over the age of ten may wear and use metal skates in the capitol building in Arkansas.

Sled coasting on highways in Vermont is illegal if it is considered dangerous to any travelers.

Why does Muskogee, Oklahoma, not have a major league baseball team? Perhaps it is because there is an ordinance forbidding any member of a ball team to hit a ball over the fence or out of the park.

It's against the law in Wentachee, Washington, to play baseball in a public place. The law also extends to throwing apples to and fro in alleys. That too is illegal.

If you play hopscotch on the sidewalk in Missouri on Sunday, you will be in violation of the law.

Gone Hunting

You are forbidden to hunt or kill a deer while swimming in Florida.

The only game you are allowed to shoot from a moving car in Tennessee are whales.

It is illegal to hunt buffalo on the parade ground in Fort Hauchuca, Arizona.

Elk are not to be hunted on Main Street in Ouray, Colorado.

In Los Angeles, California, it is illegal to hunt moths under a street light.

You must have a hunting license to catch mice in Cleveland, Ohio.

You cannot pursue wildlife "in or on a motor vehicle or by use of its lights" nor can you "take wildlife from a public highway."

You cannot catch migratory game birds from a motor vehicle or aircraft.

Flowers

It is against the law in Pueblo, Colorado, to permit a dandelion to grow within city limits.

No Sneezing, Laughing, or Any Such Thing

Gargling in public is against the law in Louisiana.

The National Association of Broadcasters forbids any scenes in which someone is gargling.

It is illegal to expectorate against the wind in Sault Ste. Marie, Michigan.

Blowing your nose in public is against the law in Waterville, Maine.

In the state of Nebraska, it's forbidden to sneeze in public. And in Omaha, it's illegal to burp or sneeze in church.

San Francisco has outlawed the purchase and sale of kerchoo powders and stink balls.

Slippery When Wet

A local ordinance in Brewton, Alabama, forbids the use of motorboats on city streets.

It is against the law in South Carolina to crawl around the public sewer system without a written permit from the proper authorities.

In the state of Vermont, it is illegal to whistle underwater.

There is a law in Lake Charles, Louisiana, making it illegal for a rain puddle to remain on your front lawn for more than 12 hours.

Durango, Colorado, forbids daytime swimming in either a pool or river.

Swimming in the nude in the waters within the corporate limits of Spring Valley, New York, is not allowed between the hours of 5 a.m. and 8:30 p.m.

If you're weeping on the witness stand in a Los Angeles courtroom, you can be found guilty of misconduct.

A lawyer in Indianapolis, Indiana, asked a criminal court judge for permission to call in a psychiatrist to examine a jury member in a robbery case. The request was denied because there is no statutory requirement that a juror be sane.

Legal Eagles

A law in Maine calls for a legal hunting season on attorneys.

In 1981, Georgia officials were poring through the statutes, and they discovered a law that allowed pensions to Confederate widows. During that week, the last widow died, and they repealed the law.

In 1985, a legislator in Arizona proposed a law

that each candidate have to take an IQ test and the results be posted on the ballot.

Bridgeport, Connecticut, passed a law stating that a city cannot go into bankruptcy. Then a legislator attempted to pass a law that would dissolve the city and divide it into its contiguous suburbs.

Each year the mayor of Danville, Kentucky, is obligated to appoint three intelligent housekeepers to the Board of Tax supervisors.

Rushville, Illinois requires a quorum at its city council meetings. If there isn't a quorum, the police are authorized to go out and arrest members of the council and drag them to meetings.

Coming Up Short . . .

A legislator in Maryland who was sensitive about his small stature had the broadcasting of singer-songwriter Randy Newman's song "Short People" outlawed on public radio.

And speaking of short . . . a legislator in Arkansas proposed that the state provide growth hormones to dwarfs.

Banned Books

The following books have been banned at one time or another:
- *Merriam-Webster Collegiate Dictionary* for obscene words in Carlsbad, New Mexico.
- *The Exorcist* in Aurora, California
- *Slaughterhouse-Five* is now on library book-

shelves, but notices will be sent to the parents of any child borrowing the book in Island Trees, New York
* *The Stepford Wives* in Warsaw, Indiana
* *Dog Day Afternoon* in Vergennes, Vermont
* *One Flew over the Cuckoo's Nest* in St. Anthony, Idaho
* *Catch-22* in Strongsville, Ohio
* *Down These Mean Streets* in Queens, New York
* *Playboy* and *Penthouse* magazines in Clay County, Mississippi
* *Ms.* magazine was ordered removed from high school libraries, but was saved by a court order in Contra Costa County, California

Sexual references in *Hamlet* were removed by many publishers.

Publishers have also removed references to drinking and lechery in *Macbeth*.

In the state of New Mexico, 400 words of "sexually explicit material" were eliminated from *Romeo and Juliet*.

Politics as Usual

An old law in Kansas prohibits politicians from handing out cigars on Election Day.

If you interrupt a speaker on Decoration Day in Ohio, you are subject to a $25 fine. (Publicly playing croquet or pitching horseshoes within one mile of the speaker's stand is considered an interruption.)

Corruption at Its Finest

There's an old law in Virginia entitled: "An Act to Prevent Corrupt Practices of Bribery by Any Person Other Than a Candidate."

So Sue Me!

You cannot sue the federal government unless you get the government's permission. There are also several states you cannot sue without their permission. (This dates back to the days of sovereignty, when one couldn't sue the sovereign or any of his agents.)

In the state of Oregon, it is illegal to require a dead person to serve on a jury.

Can children sue their mother for damage suffered as a result of negligence during the time she was pregnant with them? Yes, if the child resides in Illinois.

In Vermont, you can collect damages if another person cuts down your tree or defaces your logs.

On the Foreign Front

It's illegal in Sweden to train your seal to balance a ball on its nose.

In former East Germany, there was an anti-spy law forbidding you to wave good-bye to somebody from a train window. It could be construed as code.

This is not a duck law, but in Iceland anybody can

practice medicine, providing he/she hangs a sign that reads Scottulaejnir, which means "Quack Doctor."

There was a time in Cambodia when it was illegal to insult a rice plant.

In the Balanta tribe of Africa, a law states that a bride must remain married until her wedding gown has worn out. If she's desperate to get it over with quickly, she must wait at least one month before ripping up her wedding dress.

If a man in Greece is caught kissing a woman in public—even if the woman is his wife—he can get the death penalty.

In the 1950s, it was illegal for a flying saucer to land in the vineyards of France. It's okay now.

Male members of the Army are prohibited from carrying umbrellas to the Pentagon on a rainy day. However, female members of the Army can use umbrellas, and so can members of the Air Force and the Navy.

Screwy Law Contest

A number of years ago the Connecticut Department of Consumer Protection sponsored a "There Ought to Be a Law" contest. Here are some of the screwy laws that people found:
- In addition to smoking and non-smoking sections, restaurants must have nose-blowing and non–nose-blowing sections.
- It's illegal to sell boxes of cereal or bags of potato chips unless they are full.

- It's against the law to serve soda that has no fizz.
- All hamsters must come with a guarantee.
- "Have a nice day!"—Now what could be wrong with that? It's illegal to use those words if you're delivering bad news.
- If you're going to bare it all on a nude beach, you'd better weigh less than 125 pounds.
- If you leave your manure on a public highway, it will automatically become public property.
- Every law should be written in plain language and should be 50 words or less.
- Patients who are kept waiting in a doctor's waiting room may charge the doctor for their time.

II.
RIDICULOUS LAWSUITS

Train Trouble

In Jamestown, North Dakota, two men sued a railroad company for $10,000. Their train was behind schedule and got them to the racetrack too late to collect the winnings from the daily double.

The Case of the
Haunted Home Buyer

Guy, a former city dweller, had signed the papers, deposited $32,500 as a down payment—and was looking forward to village life. The historic town was rich in folklore, including a few "haunted" houses. What Guy didn't realize was that one of those houses was his.

Guy' first clue came when his architect refused to work on the place, on the grounds that it was ghost ridden. Then he discovered what Penelope, the seller, had failed to mention: that a round-cheeked little wraith in revolutionary dress had been hanging around the house for years.

Penelope had written all about it in the local papers and *Reader's Digest*. The ghost was perfectly cheerful, she reported. The worst it had done was eat a ham sandwich.

But Guy wasn't about to pay $650,000 to share his ham sandwich. Cancel the sale! He cried. I want my deposit back! And he sued both Penelope and the realtor.

Was Guy's ghost real? It didn't matter, the Appeals Court found. The fact that Penelope made the story public meant that "as a matter of law, the house is haunted." Its eerie reputation affected both its value and its resale potential, the court ruled, and Guy had a right to know about that.

What about "caveat emptor," or buyer beware, argued the defense. That was the going rule in real estate transactions (and a uniquely appropriate phrase in this case).

It is up to the buyer to find any problem conditions through a "reasonable inspection of the premises," the court noted. But in a case like this, as the judge put it, "Who you gonna call?" Do you take a psychic along with the structural engineer and the termite man on every home inspection? The very notion, the court ruled, should be "laid quietly to rest."

Stick 'Em Up

An unemployed poet in Port Said, Egypt, was in love with a bank teller and sent her love letters for several years. Mustafa Hazez received no replies from the teller, and decided to be more aggressive. He went to the bank and approached the teller with a gun and a love letter, demanding that she declare her love for him or hand over all the money in her drawer. She gave him the money and he was brought up on charges.

Ruling: Hazez was, of course, convicted of robbery and sentenced to jail. He was given a suspended sentence, however, on the grounds of temporary insanity.

This Is No Gag

Grace worked as a receptionist in a doctor's office where doughnuts were routinely brought in for the staff. One morning a doughnut made her ill. Grace induced vomiting, putting a pen down her throat, and accidentally swallowed the pen. She was rushed to the hospital and operated on, but was unable to work for three weeks. Grace filed for workers' compensation.

Ruling: Workers' compensation was granted by a district court judge. The Appeals Court reversed the decision, stating that: "Putting a pen down one's throat to induce vomiting is a risk. It isn't an occupational hazard of a receptionist in a doctor's office."

Iced

Parviz Mahin, a janitor at a bus depot in Ankara, Turkey, found a bag of precious stones worth $7.3 million. A Good Samaritan, he returned the stones to the jeweler. The jeweler didn't offer any reward. Mahin asked the jeweler for a small diamond ring for his wife. The jeweler refused, and Mahin took a ring. The jeweler pressed charges.

Ruling: Mahin had to spend six years in jail.

Where There's a Will . . .

In Mahdia, Tunisia, a 67-year-old philanthropist died, leaving his worldly goods to his wife, nine children, 13 grandchildren, aunts, uncles, nieces, nephews, friends, business associates, mailman, secretary, etc. He didn't, however, include his gardener or his barber. They've contested the will.

Ruling: The case is pending, and so far no one's collected a cent.

Shoplifting at Bargain Prices

A 32-year-old woman in Rutland County, Vermont, was picked up for shoplifting in a supermarket. She had helped herself to $101.49 worth of batteries, cigarettes, doughnuts, and videotapes. The woman was charged with a felony, punishable by up to 10 years in jail. Her public defender filed a motion asking the court to reduce the theft to a misdemeanor, which was punishable by a maximum of six months in jail. Apparently the threshold for a felony charge is $100 and the public defender claimed that the batteries and doughnuts were on sale, so the theft totaled only $97.37, just under the $100 threshold.

Ruling: The judge "bought it." The woman's charges were reduced to a misdemeanor.

Divorce Court

Marshfield, Wisconsin: When the couple married, he promised to pay her $1 for each kiss as long as they remained married. She sued him for divorce and asked the court for an award of $3000 in back payments.

Susanville, California: She sued him for divorce because he sold the kitchen stove in order to feed his liquor habit. He owned up to the fact that he did sell the stove, but begged the court for leniency because she didn't miss the stove for two weeks.

Pendleton, Oregon: She sued him for divorce because he never gave her Christmas presents. He claimed to be confident that Santa would bring them.

Winnemucca, Nevada: She snatched a letter from the postman that was in her husband's handwriting. When she opened the letter, she realized it was a love letter to another woman. She sued for divorce and won but had to pay a fine of $20 for tampering with the mail.

Strawberry Plains, Tennessee: She petitioned the court for divorce because she served steak and onions for dinner regularly. The problem was that he ate the steak and left her the onions.

Canon City, Colorado: She sued him on the grounds that he forced her to hide under the dashboard of his automobile whenever he passed a girlfriend.

Price, Utah: He petitioned the court for a divorce

because she insisted on hanging the pictures of her four ex-husbands over the bed.

Point Charlotte, Florida: He filed for divorce immediately after they'd taken their vows. Why? Immediately after their I do's, she took him to her favorite bar and said to the bartender: "I told you I'd marry him. Now give me the $50."

Montevideo, Minnesota: He sued her for divorce on the grounds that she didn't love him. It seems he fell down the basement steps and was sprawled on the floor in a semi-conscious state. She rushed to the scene and said, "While you're down there, put some coal in the furnace."

Huntingburg, Indiana: They met through a lonely-hearts advertisement and married before they had actually seen each other. She claimed to be five feet tall and 118 pounds, but she was actually six feet tall and weighed 300 pounds. He sued for divorce on the grounds of false advertising.

Platteville, Wisconsin: He filed for divorce after her plane trip. It seems she took out travel insurance and named their dog as beneficiary.

Grants, New Mexico: He sued her for divorce because of her extramarital affairs. The court blamed the husband, claiming that he knew of her yen for other men and should have "exercised a peculiar vigilance over her."

Rock Springs, Wyoming: Right after they had tied the knot, she admitted that she had married him for his money. He angrily filed for divorce. However, his divorce was denied because the judge explained,

"The game laws of the state provide no closed season against this kind of trapping."

Barbara sued Timothy for divorce on the grounds that he did all the housework and cooking. Barbara wasn't allowed to shop, clean house, or slave over a hot stove in the 13 years they were married. She hated living on a pedestal and charged Timothy with cruelty.

Ruling: She lost! The judge ruled that Timothy "has been tactless, not cruel."

Lee and Roberta had been married for 40 years when he took up with another woman. A divorce suit followed. Lee argued that it was all Roberta's fault because she had nagged him during their entire marriage and her "harassment, accusations, and nagging" caused him to fly into the arms of another.

Ruling: The Appeals Court ruled that after 40 years, he was carrying this a little too far. However, Roberta did not get alimony; that was the price she had to pay for the tongue lashings.

Fred and Olga were married only a month when Fred filed for divorce. He claimed the marriage should never have taken place. He was drunk at the wedding, having tippled two gallons of beer. During an argument, his 250-pound wife knocked him to the floor and sat on him for 10 minutes. He sued for divorce on the grounds of "cruel and inhuman treatment." Olga claimed that Fred wasn't pushed, rather that he fell and she sat in his lap.

Ruling: The judge granted Fred the divorce.

A woman in Crawfordsville, Indiana, sued for divorce. She claimed her husband had a habit of bringing his friends into their bathroom while she was in the tub.

A woman in France was granted a divorce after she told the judge that her husband played the bagpipes and made her keep time with a fly swatter.

The Case of the 'Healing Explosion'

It sounded like the answer to a retired schoolteacher's prayer: a faith-healing session that would finally cure her aching back. And, sure enough, when Ethel got up on stage with the Hill of Faith evangelists, she was so overcome by the "Healing Explosion" that she fainted dead away.

But the evangelists, Herbert and Joy, didn't have their act quite together that day. When Ethel went into her swoon, the designated "catchers" moved in, lunged, and missed. Ethel landed with a crack, fracturing the very spine that everybody was trying to heal.

It was kind of like a doubles tennis match, said the attorney for Hill of Faith; you know, when both players come running and nobody actually connects with the ball? Ethel was not amused. It was the federal court, not the tennis court, that she was interested in.

At the trial, the jury sided with her, ordering Herbert and Joy to fork over $300,000 for their fumble.

The Case of
the Terrible Golf Shot

Betty had just putted out at the sixth hole and was standing a few feet from the green when a golf ball came sailing down from regions unknown and conked her right on the head. The source of the missile: Rudy, located so far from Betty that you wouldn't have guessed there would be any danger. And there wouldn't, if Rudy hadn't made such a dreadful shot. Rudy's partner, Bob, had even told him that the coast was clear before he took the swing.

Nursing her injured cheekbone, Betty took both Rudy and Bob to court. There, she ran into an unexpected rule of law: the "ambit of danger zone"—the area where an onlooker might reasonably get beaned—you can collect damages, on grounds that you should have been warned. But if the ball comes at you from far afield, there's nothing you can do.

It came down to how far away Betty was from Rudy and Bob. The judge heard all the arguments—but before the case came to trial, the lawyers decided to take a swing at settling it among themselves.

The Case of the Erupting Toilet

When the septic system goes haywire, no place is safe—not even the executive washroom. That's what Alan, a bank president, discovered as he was sitting on the toilet in the executive washroom in his own bank.

Alan was minding his own business when, suddenly, a geyser of sewage-filled water "came blasting up out of the toilet with such force it stood him right up," as his attorney put it. The geyser ended as quickly as it began—but not before drenching Alan in more than 200 gallons of raw sewage.

This would have been bad enough, but then the press got wind of the story. That was the end of Alan's dignity. So he did what any red-blooded, sewage-soaked businessman would do: sue the building's construction company for damages. There ought to be some compensation, said his attorney, for the "humiliation and embarrassment" Alan suffered as his story seeped all over town.

Alas, the jury, though sympathetic, couldn't be talked into blaming the construction company. Alan was disappointed, but not enough to pump up an appeal.

The Case of the Butchered Ice Cream

Clarence worked in the kitchen of a cruise ship, filling ice cream orders for the ship's waiters. He had scooped his way down to the middle of a $2^1/2$-gallon tub one day when he reached a patch of ice cream that was "hard as a brickbat."

Clarence took an 18-inch razor-sharp butcher knife and was chipping away at the icy stuff when the knife slipped. He cut his hand—so badly that he lost two fingers. Inadequate tools to perform the task safely! Clarence cried, and he proceeded to sue the shipping company.

A jury awarded Clarence $17,500, but the Appeals Court reversed the decision. Honestly now, who could have guessed that Clarence would use a butcher knife to chip the ice cream? The judge reasoned.

The case of the butchered ice cream made it all the way to the U.S. Supreme Court, which found in favor of Clarence after all. Someone should have transferred the ice cream out of the deep freeze earlier to soften it before serving, the Court ruled. Clarence shouldn't have been stuck with the "totally inadequate" scoop, and, yes, the employer should have foreseen that he "might be tempted to use a knife to perform his task with dispatch."

The Case of the Fallen Star

Alice just knew she was going to be a famous opera star, she would dream about it on her way to singing lessons. She must have been dreaming about it the day she walked through a construction zone—because she stepped right into a hole and fell on her head.

Naturally, Alice sued the construction company. But this wasn't your typical "slip-and-fall" case. Alice sang the blues not just about her fractured leg, but about the bump on her head . . . which injured her ear . . . which messed up her hearing . . . which drove her sense of pitch right out the window.

There wasn't a dry eye in the jury, as Alice, her voice teacher, her opera coach, and her doctor described her tragic fate. Never mind that the young singer hadn't made her debut yet. Never mind that, according to another doctor, her hearing had been out of whack for years.

The jury awarded Alice $50,000—a mere token compared to the millions she would have made as the next Maria Callas, but still, not bad. However, it was not to be: The construction company appealed and the judge said, Stop the music!! Fifty thousand is a mite rich for someone who has more high hopes than bookings, he told Alice. You can have $20,000.

The Case of the Wandering Navel

When he woke up from his cosmetic surgery, Miles discovered some good news and some bad news. The good news was that the bulk had disappeared from his belly. The bad news: There was a big scar there instead—and his belly button wasn't where it was supposed to be.

You never told me this might happen! Miles cried out to Dr. Adam, the plastic surgeon. Miles had gone to see the doctor about a "liposuction" (vacuum-type fat removal), and Dr. Adam had recommended "abdominoplasty" (surgical trimming of fat and skin) as well. According to Miles, there had been no mention of scars or dislocated navels.

So he sued Dr. Adam for negligence. I've suffered "permanent disfigurement, embarrassment, pain of body and mind, and loss of income," he complained. I'm going to need to have this fixed; nobody ought to go through life with his belly button off-center!

Miles wanted a jury trial—but he and Dr. Adam managed to sit down quietly in the waiting room and stitch up their differences themselves.

The Case of Bubba
the Beer-Drinking Boar

Bubba was a big, fat, ferocious-looking wild pig—to most people. But to his owners, Clyde and Norma, he was a beloved pet who lived in their backyard and dined on chocolate and beer. They had found Bubba (who looked boar-like but was actually a javelina) on a hunting trip and raised him from babyhood.

All this was in violation of a state law against the keeping of game animals, and the sight of Bubba did startle a neighbor or two. Wildlife officers eventually learned of the matter and came to seize Bubba. Norma got out her shotgun, but to no avail—Bubba was released in a no-hunting area and Clyde and Norma went to trial.

The judge found the couple not guilty of harboring a wild animal, on the grounds that Bubba was no longer "wild." That was a technicality, according to the assistant attorney general. However mild his manner, he said, Bubba was born wild and wild he would always be. But the ruling was enough for Clyde and Norma. They immediately sued for $500,000 for their "pain and suffering."

The District Court judge ruled that Clyde and Norma couldn't collect damages for the loss of Bubba since they had no legal right to him in the first place. But the judge did allow the case to go to trial on a Fourth Amendment issue that had to do with the game wardens illegally walking through the couple's house to the backyard rather than going around it. Yet since Clyde himself had suggested that route, the jury found that it was reasonable for the officers to walk through the house.

Bubba was never seen or heard from after his release, but by that time he had become a big media celebrity. As the assistant attorney general said, "Around here, you've gotta love anybody called 'Bubba'."

The Case of the Slippery Saddle

On vacation at the Rocking Z Ranch, Nancy took a tumble off her horse. She got up, brushed herself off—and filed a product liability suit against the ranch for furnishing her with "defective and dangerous goods."

The ranchers admitted that the horse had a tricky habit of expanding its chest while it was being saddled, which made the saddle tend to wobble sideways. But this was not a dangerous animal, they insisted—"fractious," perhaps, but not dangerous.

The judge agreed. He also nixed Nancy's attempt to classify the matter as a product liability case. A horse and saddle do not constitute a "product," he wrote. "Clearly, no person ever designed, assembled, fabricated (except the Greeks at Troy), produced, constructed, or otherwise prepared a horse."

The Case of
the Limping Lovebird

It was mating season, and Lulu the parrot had a hot a date with Max at the Bird World aviary. Then suddenly, in the middle of breeding, Lulu turned up one day without three of her toes. The female macaw kept falling off her perch, and amorous activity screeched to a halt.

Lulu's owner, Erik, blamed Bird World. He claimed the aviary was so cold that Lulu had lost her toes to frostbite. But according to the aviary staff, it was more likely that she'd lost them to Max. Breeding parrots often got aggressive enough to bite each other's toes, they said.

Erik wasn't buying that explanation. He'd had big plans for Lulu and Max, whose offspring were supposed to be worth $2,000 apiece. So he filed suit against Bird World for $420,000—including compensatory damages of $170,000 for the eighty-five chicks Lulu might have had.

But the judge wouldn't allow the jury to calculate the chicks-that-might-have-been in the decision-making. Erik—his feathers seriously ruffled—won just $800 for the depreciation in Lulu's value.

The Case of the Cat in the Coffin

Marie, a housewife, was distraught when her pet poodle passed on. She called an animal funeral home, bought a satin-lined casket, and arranged for a proper burial.

But when Marie wanted a last peek before her pet was lowered into the grave, she got the shock of her life. There in the casket, in place of her poodle, was a dead cat.

Marie filed suit, on grounds that she had suffered from "shock, mental anguish, and despondency."

The judge was sympathetic and ordered the vets who had lost track of the poodle to pay Marie $700. In his ruling, the judge endeared himself to animal lovers when he wrote, "A pet is not just a thing, but occupies a special place somewhere in between a person and a piece of personal property."

The Case of the Chain-Link Canines

Lisa was strolling down the sidewalk when she was startled by a pair of dogs leaping and barking loudly behind a chain-link fence. Taken aback, the teenager darted into the street—and was struck a blow by an oncoming car.

Then Lisa struck a few blows of her own. She sued the driver of the car. She sued the owners of the "vicious" dogs. For good measure, she even sued the dog owners' next-door neighbor for not keeping the bushes and shrubs along the sidewalk properly clipped on behalf of pedestrians.

By the time the case reached an appeals court, the driver and the neighbor had been cleared—but Lisa was still trying to bring the dog owners to heel. Sorry, said the appellate judge. "Even if the dogs had been barking or jumping against the fence, such activities are quite common for a dog," he noted. And the idea of keeping a dog completely out of public sight or hearing "offends common sense."

The Case of Grandma's Geese

Everybody knew that Nellie's pet geese had their nasty side. But Mike, Nellie's grandson, wasn't worried the day he dropped by for a visit. He was more concerned about Nellie herself, who was ailing.

When Mike stepped inside the fenced yard, however, the two geese and their three goslings saw red. They rushed at Mike, their necks outstretched. When he turned to run, he tripped and fell, cracking two fingers and a wrist.

When Mike got the doctor bills from his goose attack, it seemed only reasonable to send them to his grandmother's insurance company. No way! Said the insurance company. You knew those geese were aggressive, and you assumed the risk when you walked in the gate.

Mike had only one option left: to sue his grandmother for $30,000. No hard feelings, he told Nellie, it's the insurance I'm after. In the end, though, he withdrew his suit, and grandma passed her geese along to a friend.

The Case of the Hen-Pecked . . . er, Parrot-Pecked . . . Husband

City police had a real troublemaker in Anita. Not only did she let her dogs run loose in the park, but she kept on feeding the pigeons there. Sergeant Tom had scolded her twice, and the third time, he issued a citation—or tried to. Anita refused to give her name and address (You know darned well who I am, she said), so the only course left was to arrest her.

Anita's two dogs and the parakeet she "happened to have in hand" wouldn't fit in a jail cell, so Sergeant Tom and Officer Sheila escorted her home first. When Anita's husband, Tony, heard about the arrest, he swore and punched Officer Sheila. Since Tony—and Anita, too—had a reputation as a black-belt karate expert, the officers figured they'd better call for help.

By the time the paddy wagon got there, they had subdued Tony and he was bleeding about the head.

I was clobbered by a pair of handcuffs! Tony claimed. You were clobbered by your own parrot, said Sergeant Tom. It landed on your head in the middle of the fight and started pecking.

While the police were hauling Tony to the paddy wagon, Anita locked them out of the house. They had to kick the door in to take her into custody, and Tony and Anita spent the night in jail.

The counts against Anita were severe: littering (dropping bird seed on the ground), feeding birds, allowing her dogs to run unleashed, and resisting arrest. The judge convicted her on the leash charge but let her and Tony off on the rest. Feeding pigeons was okay by the current park rules, he reminded Sergeant Tom, whose rule book happened to be eight years out-of-date.

Now, it was Tony and Anita's turn. They filed suit for assault, battery, false arrest, and malicious prosecution. A month before the trial, the city offered them $42,000 to settle the matter. That wasn't enough for Tony and Anita—but it should have been: The jury only awarded them $25,000.

And that wasn't enough for Tony and Anita's lawyers. They wanted nearly $50,000 in fees for the 332 hours they had spent on the case. Ridiculous, said the city. Such a simple case didn't justify all that time (most of which was racked up after the settlement offer); the most the lawyers deserved was $5,000. The case went through several appeals before the fee issue finally came home to roost . . . er, rest.

The Case of the Fresh-Baked Rat

Mildred ordered a loaf of bread from her local A&P. When the delivery boy got to her door, he handed her the package and gave her a message from the store manager: You'd better open it while I am here."

When Mildred opened her package, what she found was not white, whole-wheat, or rye, but a dead rat. In front of the delivery boy's eyes, she fainted and fell "with great force to the floor." In her ensuing lawsuit, Mildred claimed she had suffered "excruciating physical pain and mental anguish."

Evidence showed that the dead rat had been "carelessly substituted" for the loaf of bread by the store manager. (Apparently he had another customer who appreciated such waggish practical jokes.) "I am sorry," he told Mildred's husband, "I sent your wife the wrong package." The court awarded Mildred damages for injuries and court costs.

The Case of the Spy who Came in from the Trunk

Faced with growing evidence that his wife, Elaine, was having an affair, Chuck decided to check out the matter personally. One night when she was going out, he armed himself with a flashlight and screwdriver and hid in the trunk of her car.

Elaine stopped to pick up her lover, Joe. Then the

two parked and moved into the backseat. Chuck leaped out of the trunk and tried to climb into the car to attack his rival. But Joe scrambled out and took the offensive: He hit Chuck on the head, knocked him to the ground, and drove off with Elaine.

When Chuck came to, he found that his wife had abandoned him but his guardian angel hadn't. There on the ground beside Chuck was a pair of men's slacks, which Joe had kicked off the floor of the car during the struggle. In a pocket was Joe's wallet and ID, along with a handwritten note from Elaine.

In the ensuing divorce case, the judge wrote: "The best of [Elaine's] evidence in denial of the charge is only slightly less incredible than [Joe's] explanation as to how he came to be trouserless in the lady's car."

The Case of the Suspect Belch

When the police saw Scott "driving erratically" one night, they pulled him over. Scott agreed to a breath-alcohol test, and down at the station he got his instructions: No burping, belching, or otherwise "contaminating the oral cavity" for twenty minutes to ensure an accurate test.

The twenty-minute waiting period went by, and Scott stepped up to the machine—and belched. This meant another twenty-minute wait, said the police, and there'd better not be any more rule-breaking or they'd put Scott down as refusing the test. Fifteen minutes passed. Scott belched again. Shortly after that, he had his license revoked.

I apologize, said Scott, but please—I didn't do it on purpose! Anyone would have a tendency to belch after drowning a couple of beers and hot dogs, his attorney pointed out. But to the court, Scott's belching smacked of "an attempt to kill time to allow the alcohol to dissipate from his system."

The State Supreme Court agreed. "The question before us is whether a voluntary burp can constitute a refusal to submit to a breath-alcohol test," wrote the judge. The answer: Scott had indeed burped away his license.

The Case of the Low-Gear Lemon

Barely out of the showroom door, Paulette began to wonder if buying her brand-new car was such a good idea. The car had gone less than a mile when it stalled at a traffic light. It stalled again after 15 feet—and kept on stalling at every stop sign from then on. Halfway home, Paulette couldn't get the car to run in "drive" at all and called her husband, Cyril in a panic. Cyril limped the car home in "low-low." The fastest it would go was 10 miles an hour.

Cyril stomped to the phone and called his bank to cancel the check for the car; then he called the dealer. You sold me a lemon! He cried. The sale's cancelled!

But Randy, the dealer, felt this car was salvageable.

He towed it into his shop, replaced the dead transmission with one from a showroom model, and told Cyril: All fixed!

You don't get it, Cyril replied. I don't want this car, fixed or not; the sale's cancelled. But Cyril and Paulette still needed a car, and before long they were making a deal with Randy for the next year's model. I'll sell it to you, said Randy, but first we have to "credit" you for the other one. Cyril refused. How many times do I have to tell you that sale was cancelled, he said.

Randy wanted the balance he felt Cyril owed him, Cyril wanted his deposit back, and that's how the two wound up in court. We had signed a contract, Randy argued, and that mean Cyril "accepted" the car. But the court found that no amount of fine print could make up for a lemon as sour as this one. Every buyer has the right to assume his new car's going to run, the judge noted. When it's "practically inoperable" right out of the showroom and the buyer calls at once to cancel, the deal is definitely off.

The Case of the Runaway Cab

When Ray and Roy pulled a pistol on him in a back alley, Oliver handed over his money. But when the muggers ran off with the loot, Oliver ran off right after them. He was closing in on Roy when the thief spotted a taxicab waiting at the curb and jumped in.

Move! Roy growled to George, the cabdriver, and nudged him with the pistol. George eased the cab into traffic. But he hadn't gone more than 15 feet when he spotted Oliver in hot pursuit in the rearview mirror. Stop! Thief! Oliver was yelling. A little posse of bystanders began running and yelling right along with him. Soon, they were gaining on the slow-moving taxi.

George started to tremble. Do as I say or I'll blow your brains out! Roy snarled. But George had a better idea. Throwing his cab out of gear, he yanked on the emergency brake to send Roy off-balance, flung open the door, and hit the ground running. He was well down the block before he even bothered to look back.

What George saw when he did look back was this: The cab, abandoned by Roy as well, had run up onto the sidewalk and collided with Gladys and her two children. Their injuries were slight, however, and Roy was apprehended, hiding out in the cellar of a nearby hospital.

George thought his troubles were nearly over—until he got a call from Gladys's lawyer. Shame on you for abandoning your cab! We're suing for negligence, he was told.

Happily for George, the judge had a different idea of negligence. "The test," he pointed out, "is what reasonably prudent men would have done under the same circumstances." And when you're at the point of a gun, he found, the prudent thing is to try and save your own skin. Case dismissed.

The Case of
the "Ode on a Damaged Tree"

When a car struck and damaged his "beautiful oak tree," Elsworth was so dismayed that he took the owner of the car and the woman who was driving it to court. He also wanted a judgment against the insurance company covering the vehicle.

Elsworth got nowhere with the trial court. The owner and driver were immune from liability thanks to the state's no-fault insurance act, and the insurance company couldn't be dragged in because Elsworth hadn't gotten the procedure right.

So Elsworth appealed the case. Though the verdict was no different, he did inspire the judge, J.H. Gillis of Michigan, to write a poetic opinion on behalf of the three-justice panel:

We thought that we would never see
A suit to compensate a tree.
A suit whose claim in tort is prest
Upon a mangled tree's behest;
A tree whose battered trunk was prest
Against a Chevy's crumpled crest;
A tree that faces each new day
With bark and limb in disarray;
A tree that may forever bear
A lasting need for tender care.
Flora lovers though we three,
We must uphold the court's decree.

The Case of the Lost Lottery

Charlene was starting her New Year off with a bang: On December 30, she won $3 million in the state lottery. Five seconds later, she lost it.

In a live telecast, Charlene spun the "Big Spin" wheel and watched open-mouthed as the ball landed in her number. "You're a winner!" shrieked the announcer. The lights flashed and Charlene began to celebrate.

Moments later, the announcer tapped her on the shoulder and told her she wasn't a required winner after all. The ball hadn't stayed in the slot for the required five seconds, he said, and all bets were off.

Lottery officials sent Charlene a consolation check for $10,000, but she wasn't giving up her $3 million without a fight. Charlene took the state lottery to court.

During the jury trial, jury members were shown videotapes of Charlene's spin and those of other grand-prize winners. What did they find? That although the state might have had a five-second rule, it had never enforced the rule in the past—and there was no reason why it should suddenly do so now. Charlene walked away with $3 million and another $400,000 for emotional trauma.

The Case of the Warbling Churchgoer

Joanne, a parishioner of Our Lady of Sorrows Catholic Church, had a habit of singing songs that the rest of the congregation wasn't singing. It was bad enough when she sang from her pew, but when she got up and started singing through the sound system, Father Carl resorted to a lawsuit.

Joanne's singing, he said, was causing "confusion and disruption" during church services. In fact, the church had suffered "a loss of good will, spiritual tranquility, and membership."

The judge issued an injunction ordering Joanne to stop the music or risk being held in contempt of court.

The Case of "Fast Eddy," the Accountant

When Edward, an accountant and tax planner, switched on his television April 14, he got a peculiar kind of comic relief. There on "Saturday Night Live," in honor of the next day's income-tax deadline, was a skit about a tax consultant with the same name as his. The performer, Edward felt, even bore a "noticeable physical resemblance" to himself.

But any resemblance to real life ended when SNL's "Fast Eddy" began handing out "advice." Among the highlights:

"Your taxes are due tomorrow. You could wind up with your assets in a sling. So listen closely. Here are some write-offs you probably aren't familiar with—courtesy of 'Fast Eddy.' Got a houseplant? A ficus, a coleus, a Boston fern—doesn't matter. If you love it and take care of it, claim it as a dependent.

"Got horrible acne . . . use a lotta Clearasil? That's an oil-depletion allowance. You say your wife won't sleep with you? You got withholding tax coming back. If she walks out on you, you lose a dependent. But . . . it's a home improvement—write it off.

"Should you happen, while filling out your tax form, to get a paper cut, thank your lucky stars— that's a medical expense and a disability. Got a rotten tomato in your fridge? Frost ruined your crops—that's a farm loss. Your tree gets Dutch elm disease . . . sick leave—take a deduction. Did you take a trip to the bathroom tonight? If you took one and you did business—you can write it off.

"Call me. I have hundreds of trained relatives waiting to take your call. At Fast Eddy's, we guarantee your refund will be greater than what you earned."

Edward wrote to the producers, demanding a public apology and compensation. He got only a private apology—and the dubious pleasure of watching Fast Eddy again a couple of months later. That did it, for Edward: He sued the producers and the network for defamation.

But the court found Edward's complaint just as ludicrous as the TV show he was complaining about. The "so-called tax advice" of Fast Eddy, wrote the judge, was "so extremely nonsensical and silly that there was no possibility that any person hearing [it] could take [it] seriously."

The Case of
the Suffering Sports Fan

Benjamin, teacher and coach, was a big tennis fan—but he wasn't a big fan of John McEnroe. And he made it abundantly clear one August day when he was seated courtside at a preliminary round of the U.S. Open.

Not only was Benjamin rooting openly for McEnroe's opponent, but he was cheering each time McEnroe made a fault. "Don't you have anything better to do than cheer for my opponent all afternoon?" the tennis star cried. "No!" Benjamin said, and McEnroe shouted an obscenity back.

Tempers rose until finally McEnroe strode over to Benjamin, launched into a verbal tirade, and flung his racket in the air. Then, trailing a cloud of rosin from the racket, McEnroe stalked back and resumed play. He won his match three sets to two.

A week later, he faced a $6 million lawsuit.

Benjamin claimed he'd suffered "grievous physical and mental injuries." But that was putting it a bit strongly, according to the judge. McEnroe's behavior was "shabby" and "childlike" but hardly intolerable, he found. Far from assault and battery, the worst Benjamin had suffered was a fleck or two of rosin drifting in his direction. The judge dismissed the complaint.

The Case of the Bad Polish Jokes

The movie Flashdance had one Polish joke too

many for Anna. She decided it was time to stand up for her heritage where it counted—in court.

Anna filed a class action suit against Paramount Studios on grounds of defamation, infliction of emotional distress, and infringement of Polish people's civil rights. She didn't want any damages, since she'd only suffered "psychic injury;" Anna was suing on principle, not for money. And she turned down court-appointed attorneys in favor of representing herself.

The judge studied each of Anna's theories, but found her case "couldn't be salvaged" under any of them. "At worst, the 'Polish jokes' in Flashdance indirectly disparaged the intelligence of Polish-Americans and thereby injured their general reputation in the community," he allowed.

The Case of the Cartoon Strip-Tease

The videocassette was clearly labeled *Care Bears Storybook*, but that's not what was on the tape—as Karen discovered after her four-year-old had watched the whole thing. Instead of a cartoon about teddy bears, little Sally had just witnessed a Playboy striptease.

Mind you, there were cartoons involved: The Playboy *Farmers' Daughters* video featured nude dancers with overlays of cartoon farm animals as the cheering section. But this wasn't the kind of cartoon that Karen had in mind.

Now, Sally wanted to dance like "the Care Bears video with the naked ladies." She was even telling her friends at school about it.

Karen called Blockbuster Video and let them have it. We're sorry, but it's beyond our control, said the store; but we'll give you ten free videos to make up for it.

That wasn't enough for Karen. She sued Blockbuster for "negligence and emotional distress." I want "medical and/or counseling expenses" for Sally, Karen said, and I want you to pre-screen all children's videos before renting them out.

To Blockbuster, this was taking a simple mix-up way too far. The judge agreed.

The Case of the Ten-Foot Tomato

When you're stuck with a giant metal tomato on the roof of your restaurant and you want to change your image, what do you do with the tomato? Pasquale's Restaurant came up with a great idea: Hold a contest and award it to somebody.

Alex and a bunch of his friends were dining out at Pasquale's. On a lark, Alex entered the contest to win the tomato by guessing its weight. He wrote "555 pounds" on a slip of paper, popped it in the slot, and forgot all about it.

So it came as a bit of a surprise some weeks later when Rich, the owner of Pasquale's, drove up to Alex's house with the giant tomato on the back of a flatbed truck. It seems that Alex had come within 5 pounds of the exact weight. Since he didn't have space for the thing—it was 5 feet tall and 10 feet around—the two agreed to put it in storage.

The tomato made its way to the home of John, an employee of the restaurant. Before long, John began to stew. He claimed his employer owed him money for "expenses incurred" in storing the tomato.

Alex, meanwhile, was getting phone calls from people who actually wanted to buy the tomato. When one party offered $200, Alex agreed and he sent her to Rich, who sent her to John. The buyer got frustrated at this runaround, and Alex got mad. He filed suit against Rich. Rich filed suit against John.

Fed up, the judge ordered John to return the killer tomato to the restaurant. When the restaurant returned it to Alex, he dropped his suit—and promptly sold the tomato.

The Case of the Battling Baked Goods

It was a tense moment in the bakery big leagues. The Pillsbury Doughboy, TV commercial star, was going head to head with Drox, the Hydrox cookie character, in a trademark infringement suit.

In spite of his giggles and excess weight, the Doughboy was a tough contender. Pillsbury had created him to market its rolls, and the Doughboy had been rising nicely to the occasion for more than twenty-five years. Drox was the brainchild of Sunshine Biscuits, Inc. The creamy little character came to life on TV from the filling of Hydrox cookies.

The two coexisted in peace until Drox got a facelift—and began looking a little too much like the Doughboy, according to Pillsbury. So Pillsbury filed suit (for an undisclosed amount of dough), and for a time it appeared that Drox and the Doughboy might actually slug it out in court.

But a last-minute settlement saved the day. Sunshine agreed to drop Drox (without admitting trademark infringement), and Pillsbury agreed to drop its suit.

The Case of
the Out-of-Bounds Ball Game

Kermit and his friends were playing softball in the city park when a police officer called time-out. This is a hardball field—no softball allowed, said the officer, pointing to the sign.

But Kermit wouldn't go. Cite me! He said, so the police officer wrote up a citation. Kermit refused to sign it, and the officer had to arrest him.

A freshly minted law school grad, Kermit knew just what to do next. I'm suing for damages! He declared. You violated my First, Fourth, and Fourteenth Amendment rights!

The softball game, Kermit argued, wasn't just sport—it was "symbolic speech." He and his friends were "making a statement about the right to democracy in recreation as opposed to elitism." The city, he claimed, had no business restricting softball to one area and hardball to another. Why, such an "arbitrary and invidious" distinction was downright unconstitutional.

Oh, no, it wasn't ruled the judge. It was for perfectly good safety reasons. As for Kermit's freedom of speech, he noted, what's the "message" inherent in a softball game? And if there were one, how would anybody get it? Go "convey your message" on the softball field, the judge told Kermit. You just struck out!

The Case of the Bulky Coats

Marshall, an attorney, knew how to celebrate his thirty-fifth birthday in style: at the chic Skye View Restaurant atop the city's tallest office tower. While he and his friends were waiting to be seated, the host told Marshall he'd have to check his raincoat. Marshall said he'd rather keep it with him, but the host insisted: It was restaurant policy that gentleman check their coats.

Only gentleman—not ladies? Asked Marshall, his ears pricking up. Only gentlemen, said the host. That was all Marshall needed to hear. He marched his friends out of the restaurant and filed a sex-discrimination complaint.

The restaurant claimed its policy was a "legitimate business judgment." We're not trying to discriminate against men, said the owners, but when you hang a bulky coat over the back of your chair, it gets in people's ways. If it falls on the floor—heavens, somebody could trip over it and get hurt. And everyone knows that men's coats are bulkier than women's.

Says you, argued Marshall. Everyone knows that women's coats are bulkier than men's.

After hearing both sides, the judge decided that men were getting a bum deal at Skye View and he ordered the restaurant to "cease and desist" its one-sided coat policy. He wouldn't, however, give Marshall the damages he wanted for "mental anguish."

The Case of the Smoke-Filled Rooms

Hilary, a cigarette smoker, didn't mind the no-smoking rules at work—but it was a different matter when a neighbor took her to court for smoking in her own home.

Stanley, whose apartment was directly above Hilary's, complained that the smoke from her cigarettes was oozing up through vents and cracks and driving him crazy. So, he filed a nuisance suit.

Hilary admitted to a certain amount of smoking: up to six cigarettes a day, she told the judge. But could this possibly be an "illegal activity" in her own home? The lease, she pointed out, didn't say a word about it.

Not having any hard evidence about the volume of smoke in Stanley's apartment, the judge dismissed his suit as so much hot air. The smoke from a few cigarettes, he ruled, was hardly "an annoyance of real and substantial nature."

The Case of the Nine-Hole Nuisance

Cracked windows and dents in the car were par for the course for Sylvia and her family. They lived alongside a city-owned, par-three golf course—and the duffers who played there were wreaking havoc on their lives.

Sylvia's backyard was less than 50 yards from the green on the third hole. By the time she decided to go to court, Sylvia had an impressive handicap: twenty-two dents in the family cars, three shattered windshields, and seven broken windows in the house and the garage.

Sylvia won her civil suit. The judge gave her $2,500 for property damage and $3,700 for disruption of her "quietude of domicile." But he wouldn't rule the golf course a public nuisance, and the slices and hooks continued to rain golf balls onto Sylvia's property.

Sylvia made one last stab at restoring her family's peace. She tried to get criminal charges filed against the city for 1,087 counts of reckless endangerment and 1,087 counts of criminal trespass by people and golf balls—one count for each golf ball in the four-year family collection. But it didn't work. On this claim, the court told Sylvia, you're out of bounds.

The Case of
the Poolside Cemetery

Gilbert and Denise should have had grave misgivings about their new home. Somebody had told the builder that there was an old cemetery on the site and showed him a little fenced-in area with a cross on a stick. Maybe a dog's grave, the builder thought, and he had the debris hauled off and dumped.

It wasn't until two years later, when they decided to put in a swimming pool, that Gilbert and Denise first heard of the matter. Better put a good lining in that pool, warned a neighborhood old timer. Rumor has it there's a body or two in your backyard.

Sure enough, when they checked it out, the couple learned that there had once been a graveyard on their land. So they put the chlorine on hold and called the excavator instead.

Two human graves turned up. The developer had them moved to a cemetery, but Gilbert and Denise weren't about to let this matter rest in peace. They filed suit for damages, for a host of violations including breach of contract, negligence, and fraud.

"Our lives aren't the same since we found those graves," said Gilbert and Denise. We can't sleep, we've lost weight . . . and it's creepy around here! A jury awarded them $142,600. But the trial judge took it back. That cemetery was abandoned, which means your complaints are moot, said the judge— and the Appeals Court.

The State Supreme Court, though, breathed life

back into the case. Just because a graveyard isn't a working graveyard anymore doesn't mean the poor homeowners have to put up with it, the court found. Gilbert and Denise did deserve a remedy.

The Case of the Unmowed Lawn

"But we're making hay," said Kevin and Anne when their neighbors complained about their two-foot-high front lawn. They planned to mow the grass, honest they did, said the couple. They just wanted to wait until fall, when the harvest would be mature.

That wasn't good enough for their neighbor, Darrell. Darrell and his wife had their house on the market, and the untidy mess at Kevin and Anne's was creating the wrong ambiance. In fact, Darrell felt that the two grass lovers were deliberately out to sabotage his real estate sale. So he sued them for $2.5 million.

When the case reached County Court, the judge burst out laughing and dismissed the complaint. But, as a consolation to Darrell, he ordered Kevin and Anne to cut their grass by the first of September.

That's not fall, argued the couple's attorney. The judge responded, "Fall is going to come earlier this year."

The Case of the Weed Invasion

Weeds in the yard were one thing, but when the weeds came poking through the floor in their brand-new home, Terry and Ruth called a lawyer. They'd been in the $80,000 rambler for about a year when horsetail weeds began coming up through the seams where the floors met the walls in every room of the house.

Terry and Ruth complained to the builder. He took measures to get rid of the problem, but the horsetails were stubborn as mules. Terry and Ruth were still hard at work weeding the garage at the time they decided to file suit.

The builder hadn't prepared the ground properly before pouring the slab floor, they argued, and that was how the weeds got a foothold. We want out of here, said the couple. But by the time the case reached court three years later, the judge ruled the house "habitable" and found in favor of the builder.

The Case of the Falling Acorns

Those pesky acorns that kept dropping from their neighbor's oak tree were a serious problem to Mac and Margaret. The darned things came down like a hailstorm, coating the driveway and sidewalks. A body could slip and break his neck.

Mac and Margaret complained to the neighbor, Calvin, time and again: Cut down the part that hangs over our property, they begged. "You cut it down," said Calvin. Finally the elderly couple had no choice but to sue. They took Calvin to court for "an unspecified amount of damages" and to force him to trim his tree.

That was enough to get Calvin and his chainsaw into action, and the suit was settled out of court.

The Case of the Rotten Restaurant Review

"T'aint Creole, t'aint Cajun, t'aint French, t'aint country American, t'aint good." That's how Fritz, the food critic, began his review of the new restaurant Maison de Marvin.

In his newspaper column, Fritz went on at great length about how much he didn't like Marvin's restaurant. The oysters Bienville were "a ghastly concoction," the escargots à la Marvin "pretentious failures that leave a bad taste in one's mouth." He wrote, "the poached trout under crawfish sauce, I would have named trout à la green plague."

As for the roast duck: "Put a yellow flour sauce on top of the duck, flame it for drama, and serve it with some horrible multi-flavored rice in hollowed-out fruit, and what have you got? A well-cooked duck with an ugly sauce that tastes too sweet and thick and makes you want to scrape off the glop and eat the plain duck." Fritz later called this dish "yellow death on duck."

"A travesty of pretentious amateurism . . . I find it all quite depressing," Fritz summed up. "Only the proprietor can answer the question of whose taste is on the menu. If it is his, then his restaurant is an irremedially ghastly mistake."

Having his restaurant labeled a ghastly mistake

was too much for Chef Marvin, and he sued for $2 million. You've injured my professional reputation, lost me business, and personally humiliated me, he told Fritz and his newspaper.

The review wasn't malicious, said Fritz, it was simply "fair comment." When a lower court agreed with that, Marvin appealed—but didn't do any better. Though one dissenting judge did call the review "a degrading, malicious, and unprovoked attack," the court ruled that "ordinary reasonable persons" would see it merely as "expressions of a writer's opinion."

The Case of the "Careless" Accident Victim

Little Becky was hit by a car in a street accident in her hometown. A newspaper photographer on the scene got a dramatic shot of the ten-year-old being lifted to her feet, and the picture ran in the next day's paper. The driver was found at fault in the accident, and Becky recovered from her injuries.

She and her family got a second shock, though, when they opened their Saturday Evening Post a year and a half later. There was the picture of Becky, illustrating a feature story titled "They Ask to Be Killed." The story, on the theme of pedestrian carelessness, included this splashy blurb "Do you invite massacre by your own carelessness? Here's how thousands have committed suicide by scorning laws that were passed to keep them alive."

This was too much for Becky and her family. They sued the publisher (who, as it happened, had bought the photo from a supplier of illustration material). A lower court awarded the family $5,000 for their pains, and an appeals court upheld the ruling. The original use of the photo was fine, the judge found. It had legitimate news value at that time. But its use in the Post did "exceed the bounds of privilege."

The Case of the Flyaway Skirt

Frieda, a middle-aged farmer's wife, never guessed she'd be the local pin-up girl when she took her two children to the county fair. But a hired photographer snapped a photo of Frieda in the fun house with her skirt blown up over her waist—and the local paper ran the photo on page one.

A lifelong resident of the county and a pillar of her church, Frieda was shocked when she spotted the paper on a display rack and chagrined when several of her friends mentioned it. She sued for invasion of privacy, claiming that the incident had made her "embarrassed, self-conscious, and upset" and that she "was known to cry [about it] on occasions."

The court found that Frieda's privacy had indeed been breached and awarded her damages. "We can see nothing of legitimate news value in the photograph," the judge ruled. "Certainly it discloses nothing as to which the public is entitled to be informed."

The Case of the Missing Bottle Box

As part of her hotel lobby newsstand, Genevieve sold Coca-Cola from a vending machine. A Coke employee would drop by regularly to take away the empty bottles and bring refills.

One midsummer day, Genevieve noticed that she was missing an empties box and "politely inquired" about it. Rick, the Coke man, replied "in a burst of explosive anger and in a loud and menacing voice." "You've got that case back there in the corner! I can see it from here!" he yelled.

Genevieve tried to explain that there was no empties box in the corner. She even offered to show him. But Rick would have none of it. "I don't have to go back there," he said. "You know you've got that box back there. You fool with me and I'll take that box out of here!"

Since this tiff was taking place in full view of customers, hotel workers, and "the public in general," Genevieve got so upset that she decided to sue the Coca-Cola Bottling Company—for slander. But the court let the fizz out of Genevieve's complaints. The incident, it ruled, was "at most . . . one of those stupid, unnecessary, and ill-tempered arguments which, if they should be held as constitutional slander . . . would overburden the courts."

The Case of the Purloined Porter

Cole Porter has been swiping my tunes for just about long enough, Lenny decided—and he sued the famous songwriter for copyright infringement. It wasn't Lenny's first lawsuit, not by a long shot. Over the years, he'd sued five other composers for the same offense.

Cole Porter hadn't dream up "My Heart Belongs to Daddy" all by himself, Lenny claimed. The tune came from Lenny's "A Mother's Prayer." "Begin the Beguine" came from there, too. "Night and Day" was stolen from Lenny's "I Love You Madly," and "Don't Fence Me In" was right out of "A Modern Messiah."

Lenny wanted "at least $1 million out of the millions Cole Porter is earning all out of plagiarism." When the judge asked Lenny where Porter might have heard his music in order to copy from it. Lenny pointed out that "A Mother's Prayer" had sold more than a million copies. As for the other pieces, most of them had been played at least once over the radio.

Besides, Lenny claimed, Cole Porter "had stooges right along to follow me, watch me, and live in the same apartment with me." His room had been ransacked several times, he said. How do you know Cole Porter had anything to do with it, the judge asked. "I don't know that he had anything to do with it; I only know that he could have," Lenny explained.

The district judge found Lenny's whole story fantastic and dismissed it. The Appeals Court, though, did find similarities between Lenny's music and Cole Porter's. Yes, the judge admitted, that part about the stooges was pretty weird, but "sometimes truth is stranger than fiction." It would be up to a jury to decide.

Sadly for Lenny, the jury didn't swallow his story. He appealed again—he even petitioned the U.S. Supreme Court—but finally he had to compose himself and go home.

The Case of the Vengeful Newspaper

When Virginia saw what the Gazette had printed, she was so mad she could hardly see straight. There were the profiles of all the candidates for the upcoming election, but the profile of her candidate, Kay, was garbled to the point where it made no sense.

I don't think this was completely accidental, Virginia said to herself. These guys were out to get my candidate! So she wrote an angry letter to the editor of the Gazette. To make sure her letter would run in full, she asked that it be published as a paid ad and she sent the paper a check for $560. The Gazette printed Virginia's letter. Then it turned around and sued her for libel and slander.

"A man-bites dog story!" said the Appellate judge when the case reached his court. Nobody had ever heard of a newspaper suing over its own contents. A trial judge had ruled that this couldn't be done—

but the Gazette appealed, on grounds that Virginia had "compelled" it to print her ad.

Nobody compelled anybody, the Appeals Court found. The Gazette had freely chosen to publish Virginia's statements. And as the publisher, it couldn't sue, because "it is self-axiomatic that a person cannot sue himself or herself."

The Case of the Buttock-Biting Barrister

When Ted spotted Susie in a barroom near the university, he was so overcome by her charms that he grabbed her by the hips and gave her a bite on the backside. "I meant it as a compliment," Ted claimed. As a lawyer, he should have known better. Ted soon found himself on the receiving end of a lawsuit.

The amorous bite, said Susie's attorney, broke the skin on her buttocks and caused "searing and throbbing pain." Susie couldn't even attend classes—she couldn't sit down for three days.

Ted admitted to nipping the victim, but he insisted he meant her no harm. He had already tried the technique on two other women at fraternity parties, and neither of them took him to court.

This time, however, the victim bit back. While Ted and his lawyer felt that Susie deserved only the $9 she spent on medication, the jurors awarded her $27,500 in damages.

The Case of the Squatter's Rights

His marriage was only a month old, but Billy was ready to call it quits. The ceremony shouldn't have happened in the first place, he claimed in his divorce petition: He was drunk on more than two gallons of beer at the time, and when he got cold feet, his 230-pound bride sat on him.

Pleading with the court to dissolve the union on grounds of "cruel and inhuman treatment," Billy claimed that his wife Cissie, knew darned well he was drunk when she sat on him. There was an argument, he said, during which Cissie knocked him to the ground, sat on him, and "would not allow him his freedom" for a good ten minutes.

"I did not knock him down," Cissie countered. "He stumbled and fell, and I sat on his lap. Then I told him he wasn't getting up unless we went through with it."

The judge went through with the divorce.

The Case of the Ousted Spouse

In the midst of divorce proceedings, Carol felt she couldn't tolerate Gerald's presence in their Manhattan apartment for one more minute. So she had the locks changed.

Normally, a divorce court wouldn't allow her to get away with such a move, since Gerald wasn't physically abusive. But Carol argued a different form of abuse.

Gerald hadn't taken a bath or changed his clothes

in weeks, she pointed out. In a 450-square-foot studio apartment, that was cause for drastic action. The judge agreed. "There is no reason why the plaintiff should be subjected to the extremely uncomfortable situation that prevailed prior to the defendant being locked out," he sniffed.

The Case of the Drop-In Husband

Hugh and Connie were separated . . . sort of. Hugh had moved out, but he made a habit of dropping by for dinner and some after-dinner wifely affection. Then he'd ride off into the sunset.

After three-and-a-half-years of this, Connie got fed up. I'm too old for one night stands, she told Hugh; dinner is all you're getting from now on. Hugh promptly sued for divorce—on grounds that his wife had "abandoned" him.

The court, however, wouldn't buy this logic. "You can't abandon someone who's already moved out," the judge told Hugh. Connie was perfectly justified in feeling uncomfortable with the arrangement and putting an end to it. After three-and-a-half years, there was plainly no reconciliation in the works. Hugh, ruled the court, just wanted to "continue his nocturnal comings and goings."

The Case of the Skinflint Widow

When she got the bill for her late husband's funeral, Eliza dug in her heels. They'd been separated at the time of Jake's death, she said, so she had no obligation to pay. This reasoning had not, of course, stopped her from collecting Jake's life insurance.

The undertaker sued, and the case made its way to the State Supreme Court. There, the puzzled judge found no specific law on the books to cover such situations. He had to rely on common law to find that, though a husband was responsible for his wife's funeral expenses, she was not for his.

"It regretfully appears," he noted, "that the undertakers who performed the last earthly service for Jake will have to look to a greater court than this for their reward."

The Case of the Split Windfall

Beverly was faithful to the state lottery. She bought a ticket every week, and every now and then she would win a little. Burt thought she was silly. In his view, the lottery was a waster of money that they should be saving to buy a house.

He did make one exception: When his co-workers decided to spring for some lottery tickets through an office pool, Burt went along. He knew if he refused and they won, Beverly would be hopping mad.

As it happened, the office pool did win. In fact, Burt and his buddies won the grand prize. But Beverly was hopping mad anyhow. You see, it wasn't

long after Burt's big win that the couple split up—
and Burt demanded the lion's share of the lottery
winnings.

A trial court sided with Burt, giving him 85 percent of the loot and Beverly a paltry 15 percent.
When she appealed, though, Beverly's luck began
to change.

The winning ticket was purchased with "marital
funds," the Appeals Court found, and should be
shared equally since Burt and Beverly shared
equally in the costs of their household.

Burt said he deserved more because he'd gone to
the trouble of buying the ticket. As for "marital
funds," he claimed, the dollar he used to buy the
ticket "might have been a dollar I found on the
street the day before while walking the dog."

Sorry, said the court, your winnings were more a
matter of good fortune than of anyone's special
efforts. And after Beverly had deposited her "mea-
ger" winnings into the joint account for all those
years, it was only fair for Burt, too, to share and
share alike.

The Case of the Nagging Wife

After almost forty years of marriage, Lee was
breaking loose. First he found a new love, Doreen;
then he moved out on the old one, Roberta.

Roberta asked the court for alimony. The separa-
tion, she pointed out, was the fault of the two-timing
Lee. But Lee argued that it was just as much

Roberta's fault. Her constant henpecking all those years made it plain impossible to stay married to her, he said.

Roberta's "harassment, accusations, and nagging" amounted to such "cruel treatment" that living with her was "insupportable," Lee claimed. He had a witness testify that Roberta was rude to him in public, made scenes about his affair with Doreen, and even called him "bald-headed."

That sounded pretty serious to the trial court and the Appeals Court. Both of them agreed with Lee that the breakup was partly Roberta's fault, which meant that she wasn't eligible for alimony. But the State Supreme Court found that Lee was taking a little nagging way too far.

"All spouses have faults," the court pointed out. And Roberta's faults, it found, were hardly so cruel or excessive that Lee was compelled to leave. After all, he "had tolerated his wife's tongue for nearly forty years," hadn't he?

The Case of the Missing Funds

After she married Myron, Roxanne went to work as a bookkeeper of his company, Wilson Widgets. Three years later, she wanted the job but not the husband. Roxanne filed for divorce but kept on at Wilson Widgets . . . until Myron began to suspect that his bookkeeper was making off with the funds.

You're through, Myron told Roxanne. By now she had opened a catering business on the side. But profits were poor. Roxanne claimed that she had only $140 in the bank when she went to court seeking temporary maintenance.

Myron's got more than a million bucks; why shouldn't I have some? Roxanne asked the court, and she won $2,500 a month plus costs. But Myron blew the whistle on that. We haven't cleared up the matter of Wilson Widgets' missing funds, he reminded the Appeals Court.

Myron had a fistful of documents pointing to Roxanne as the "thief"—documents totaling more than $25,000. But when his lawyer asked Roxanne about it, she pleaded the Fifth Amendment. I have the right not to incriminate myself, said Roxanne, and I'm keeping my mouth shut.

That was her privilege, the court agreed, but it put Roxanne in a "Catch-22." If she wanted support, she had to fess up about how much money she really had; if she wanted to plead the Fifth, it disqualified her for support. That's the rule, said the court.

Maybe in a really serious case, like murder, Roxanne argued, but for a silly little embezzlement? Why, my case "pales in comparison." The rule's the rule, said the court.

The Case of the Costly Non-Divorce

Sure, I'll handle your divorce, Nathan told Meg. Here's how it works: You pay me a retainer of

$15,000 to cover all the work I'm going to do. And, by the way, that $15,000 is nonrefundable.

Meg went along with it. But as luck would have it, soon after she signed the agreement, love conquered all and Meg decided to stay married. I don't need you anymore, she told Nathan.

According to his billing records, Nathan spent a total of five hours on Meg's case. At $275 an hour, she figured she owed him $1,305 and she wanted the rest back. Sorry, Nathan said. Don't you remember what I said about "nonrefundable?"

At that, Meg filed suit against her lawyer. And though Nathan claimed that his agreement was perfectly ethical, the court found otherwise.

Discounting the first eight-tenths of an hour that Nathan billed Meg because it occurred before the agreement was even signed, the court found that he was charging her what amounted to $3,571.43 an hour. A fee that was so "grossly excessive" that it was "shocking to the court's conscience."

There's no way this agreement is enforceable, the court told Nathan. On top of that, it discourages your client's absolute right to discharge you, and it doesn't exactly encourage her to reconcile, either. Give the money back, plus interest!

The Case of
the Drummed-Out Musician

Jerry was first-chair saxophone in his high-school marching band, but he had a splashier role in mind.

In his senior year, Jerry went out for drum major. He made it to the finals, but he wasn't chosen—and by this time, all the slots in the saxophone section were full.

You can play the cymbals till marching season is over, said Sam, the band director. Then you can be a saxophonist again.

This was small comfort to Jerry. In fact, the thought of cymbal-banging made him so mad that he marched into County Superior Court and filed a complaint against Sam. Not choosing me as drum major was a violation of my constitutional rights, Jerry argued. And not letting me go back to first-chair saxophone—that was a violation of my constitutional rights, too!

But the judge saw the matter a little differently. It's the band director's right to choose who plays what, the judge ruled, and he sent Jerry marching out the door.

The Case of the Teacher's Kick-Back

All was well on the preschool playground except that little Timmy wouldn't put his bicycle way. Timmy's teacher, Jenny, asked him once and the five-year-old just ignored her. When she asked him again, he threw a tantrum.

While Jenny was trying to calm Timmy down, he turned and kicked her so hard in the ankle that she fell on the ground. And that was the incident that caused Jenny to strike a blow to preschoolers everywhere: She filed suit against Timmy and his parents for $25,000.

Timmy's kick, as it turned out, packed such a wallop that Jenny was off work for months and had to have a series of operations to correct her "tarsal tunnel syndrome." For a long time, she could walk only with the aid of a cane.

There's a happy ending though. The case was settled out of court, Jenny hobbled back to the classroom, and Timmy graduated from preschool and awaits a bright future in the NFL.

The Case of the Would-Be Doctor

Patience was a nurse with a mission: to go to medical school and become a doctor. A thorough person, she applied to every medical school in her state. All seven turned her down. It wasn't that Patience was a terrible candidate—but she wasn't a terrific one, either. "There were at least 2,000 unsuccessful applicants who had better academic qualifications," said the dean of one of the medical schools.

Then Patience discovered her true calling: not medicine, but the law. She promptly filed suit against two of the schools that had rejected her, alleging (among other things) age and sex discrimination. Her case made its way to the U.S. Supreme Court and back, to no avail.

Four years later, she sued the other five schools, with no better luck. And five years after that, Patience took all seven medical schools back to court, on somewhat different legal theories but with the same underlying facts.

Give up, said the judge. He dismissed the case, awarded fees and costs to the defendants—and scolded Patience's attorney for not recognizing "an obviously lost cause."

The Case of the Lost .065

As the salutatorian of her high school class, Shelly took her grade-point average seriously . . . very seriously. One day she missed algebra class. Since she had no excuse, the teacher lowered her grade—and that meant a slip in her overall grade-point average from 95.478 to 95.413.

Now, .065 might not sound like much; but to Shelly's dad, Ralph, you start letting the little things go and pretty soon the big ones will follow. Ralph saw only one solution: to sue the school board for a million dollars.

That docked grade-point was a violation of his daughter's Fifth and Fourteenth Amendment rights, Ralph told the court. The judge consented to the reinstatement of the grade-points, but he refused to award any money. Ralph appealed the decision, hoping at least to get his attorney's fees paid—but the Appeals Court judge was so exasperated that he took the grade-points away again.

"Patently insubstantial" was how the judge saw this case.

The Case of
the Forty Billion Burgers

Matthew and Nicole passed the golden arches every day—but one day, the big sign made them do a double-take. Could McDonald's really have sold "more than 40 billion" hamburgers? Matthew asked Nicole. Let's figure it out, she replied.

According to Nicole's calculations, McDonald's would have had to sell a hamburger every second of every day for a thousand years to reach that number. They would have had to kill every cow born since the 1600s.

Aha, the two exclaimed. False advertising! And they filed suit against McDonald's.

We want the U.S. government to stop McDonald's from lying to the public, Matthew and Nicole argued. "Lies cause great mental strain on the individual as well as the nation," they explained. And we want the IRS to substantiate this claim about the forty billion burgers, they added. Come up with an income statement and we'll drop our suit—and "throw ourselves on the fairness of the Court to give us a fair percentage of the money uncollected in tax."

Alas, Matthew and Nicole came up empty-handed. The court dismissed their suit, deciding instead: You deserve a break today, McDonald's.

The Case of the Accountant's Birthday Suit

The IRS was on the trail of Craig, a self-employed accountant. Craig had hundreds of thousands of dollars in unaccounted-for bank deposits—deposits on which he had paid no income tax. After years of pursuit involving records from twenty different bank and brokerage accounts, the U.S. Tax Court finally hauled Craig in.

Craig had dozens of reasons why his deposits weren't taxable income, including one $537 item that struck the Tax Court as particularly "novel." This $537 is obviously a gift, Craig claimed. It has to be, because I put it into the bank on my birthday.

Many happy returns, said the court—tax returns, that is.

The Case of the Too-Many Taj Mahals

When your name is Trump, you've got to spend a certain amount of time defending that name from misuse. "The Donald" was no stranger to the courts. But he wasn't used to being on the receiving end of the lawsuit—and that's just where he was when Victor decided he didn't want any more Taj Mahals cluttering up the marketplace.

Victor ran a second-floor Indian eatery called the Taj Mahal. It was located in a downtown commercial zone, seated about seventy-five, and served curries, rice dishes, and the like for prices that topped out at $12.25.

Donald was opening a casino-hotel called the Trump Taj Mahal. It dominated the skyline in a seaside resort. The multi-million dollar building contained ten restaurants (none of them Indian), four cocktail lounges, 120,000 square feet of gambling parlor, and 1,250 guest rooms—the most expensive priced at $10,000 a night.

You wouldn't think that anyone could confuse these two establishments, but Victor wasn't so sure. He filed suit for infringement of his registered service mark—and for "unfair competition."

Victor, you don't own the name "Taj Mahal," the judge reminded the plaintiff. There are at least twenty-four other restaurants and seventy businesses in the United States using that name. Unless you can prove a likelihood of confusion, this suit is going nowhere. Some of my friends and patrons are confused, Victor insisted, at least eight of them. Either they're worried about my links to the Trump empire, or they want me to get them discounts.

Sorry, said the judge. "None of these people actually went to the Trump Taj Mahal . . . under the mistaken impression that it was related to Victor's restaurant," he noted. As for the unfair competition, that too proved a trumped-up charge. There was "absolutely no evidence," the judge ruled, that Donald had named his casino "with the intention of preying on Victor's commercial reputation."

The Case of
the Devilish Lawsuit

You can file suit against the Devil himself and have your day in court, Adolph found, but you won't necessarily get any satisfaction. Adolph filed a civil rights action against "Satan and his staff." The defendant, he claimed, had "on numerous occasions caused him misery" and had "placed deliberate obstacles in his path and caused his downfall."

That might well be, said the judge, but there wasn't anything he could do about it. First, he noted, "we question whether Adolph may obtain personal jurisdiction over the defendant in this judicial district." Nobody knew for sure whether Satan had his legal residence there.

The case might be considered as a class action, the judge went on, but that was going to be tough given the vast size of the "class"—and the question of whether Adolph's claims were representative of everyone else's. Finally, the judge noted, Adolph hadn't given any instructions as to exactly how the U.S. marshal was supposed to serve process on Satan and his servants.

In this case, at least, the Devil came out "not guilty."

The Case of
the X-Rated Tax Payment

When she found her property-tax bill in her mailbox, Renee looked at the due date and started to steam. The bill was so late in coming that she barely had time to get her check in before the deadline.

Renee wrote out her $250 check and rushed it to the post office—but she wasn't going to let this pass without comment. On the envelope, instead of "Walter MacKay, County Treasurer," she wrote "Walter MacKay, Bastard."

And on the check itself, Renee used the memo line to jot an explicit two-word message to Walter.

As tax collector, Walter was used to a certain amount of resentment . . . but he wasn't used to the four-letter variety. He filed a libel lawsuit against Renee. For heaven's sake, said Renee's lawyer, can't public officials take a little ribbing once in a while? But the judge was unmoved. The fine he levied on Renee was twice what she paid in taxes.

The Case of Life, Liberty, and the Pursuit of Sex

Willard believed he had a God-given right to sex—and he was willing to go to court to defend it. He sued the state for having an anti-prostitution law. "Unconstitutional!" Willard cried. He sued the city police for posing female officers as "demi-mondaines" and luring unsuspecting men. "Entrapment!" he shouted.

The authorities, according to Willard, had forced him into either abstaining from sex or becoming a criminal in order to get it.

When a lower court dismissed Willard's case, he took it to the Court of Appeals. "Patently frivolous!" hooted the Circuit Court. "Devoid of arguable merit." And the judges slapped Willard with double costs and attorneys' fees.

The Case of the Ritzy Toilet Seat

Everyone knew Norm, the plumber, by his family nickname, Ritz. When Norm invented a potty training seat, it was only natural that he name it after himself. He called his toilet seat the "Ritz-Z."

But when that name showed up on the patent applications list, a sharp-eyed attorney hopped to attention. Before he knew it, Norm was facing formal opposition from a most unlikely source: the famed Ritz Hotel in Paris.

The president of the Ritz, who flew to the United States to testify, said Norm had no business using the Ritz name. "The Ritz Hotel in Paris stands for privacy, for perfection, for discretion," he argued. The very thought of a baby's bottom coming in contact with this name—one could only pooh-pooh such a suggestion.

Norm, the plumber, stood his ground. Ritz was "the nickname everybody in his family has had for generations," he said. Besides said his attorney, "there is such a difference in the channels of trade" of the Ritz Hotel in Paris and Norm's toilet seats that no one could possibly confuse the two.

The Patent Office judge agreed, and he closed the lid on the case.

The Case Against Ronald Reagan

The judge knew it was going to be one of those days the minute he opened Leon's file. Here was a lawsuit overflowing with defendants and claims.

First, there was the matter of Ronald Reagan. Leon was suing Reagan for neglecting him, depriving him of his right to vote, causing him to be arrested, and bringing about his "civil death." The president, he added, "has acted with redundancy and malicious conduct."

Next, there was the matter of Leon's parking tickets. He had stuffed a bunch of these in the file in hopes of getting a jury to help him straighten out his fines.

Then there was the request that someone investigate White Line Fevers from Mars—not as you might think, a rock band, but a fruit company. Leon claimed W.L.F.F.M was shipping marijuana, not grapefruit, in its Mother's Day boxes. Leon had lost his trucking license after a run-in while delivering these boxes.

Just to round out the file, Leon threw in a poem he had written about birds, crickets, ants, and a monarch butterfly. The judge also found a U.S. Supreme Court form on which Leon had written, "Why isn't the 1840 mailbox still next to the 1830 one?" and "Something suspicious about that mail-box."

Law school sure hadn't prepared the judge for cases like this one. He figured he would be safe dis-missing it as a "frivolous action." But for reasons of its own, an appeals court reversed the case—and there was Leon, back to haunt the judge again.

What the heck? said the judge to himself, and he told his marshals to go ahead and serve process on President Reagan and the rest of the gang. But sud-denly, Leon wasn't holding up his end. He didn't return the judge's mail, he let deadlines go by—he "seems to have lost touch with the court, or lost interest, or both," said the judge. And he dismissed Leon v. Reagan for the last time.

The Case of the Rear-Ended Nurse

Nurse Diana had always gotten along famously with Dixie, her supervisor in the emergency room. Famously, that is, until the two joined an eight-day river rafting trip.

It seems that the great outdoors brought out a side of Dixie that nobody saw in the emergency room. She drank like a trooper. She took baths in public. To top things off, she organized a rendition of the song "Moon River" that ended with the singers "mooning" the audience. Diana said she'd just as soon butt out.

Back at the hospital, Dixie put on her little skit

again—and again Diana said no. At this point, Diana started getting bad vibes from her supervisor. Dixie was "harassing her, using abusive language, and embarrassing her in front of the other staff." Diana had always gotten high ratings before the trip, but it wasn't long afterward that she found herself jobless.

Diana wasn't about to take this sitting down, and she filed suit. The hospital claimed that since she was an "at will" (non-contract) employee, she could be fired at any time—for "good cause, bad cause, or no cause."

Not so, ruled the court. It was wrong to fire Diana for a bad cause . . . and this cause was definitely a bad cause. "We have little expertise in the techniques of mooning," wrote the judge. But "compelled exposure of the bare buttocks on pain of termination," he found, was what the indecent exposure law was there to prevent.

The Case of the Non-Affair

Sick and tired of seeing female co-workers having affairs and getting raises, Bonita filed suit because she wasn't. An attorney with the federal government, Bonita claimed her office was an offensive, unfair, and "sexually hostile" work environment for no-nonsense females like herself.

I've only gotten one promotion in five years, though I was eligible for plenty, Bonita pointed out. She also pointed a finger at these supervisors:

• Nick, admitted to having an ongoing affair with

a secretary. The secretary got three promotions, a commendation, and two cash awards.

- Kenneth had a "noticeable attraction" to a female attorney. The attorney rose three grade levels in two years.
- Paul shared long lunches, dinners, and a resort hotel room with a clerk typist. (According to Paul, they spent the night discussing the typist's "theological problems.") Within a single year, the typist got two promotions, a $300 cash award, and a perfect score on her performance appraisal.

Faced with evidence like that, the court agreed with Bonita. Her managers had "effectively harassed" her, the court found, and she deserved her promotions—as well as retroactive pay increases.

The Case of the Horrible Haircut

Glenn had a vision of the hairstyle he wanted. He had grown his hair out for more than two years in preparation, and—armed with a photo—he arrived at his local hairstyling salon.

When Glenn left the salon, he had a different vision: a $10,000 lawsuit. Gone were nearly 10 inches of his crowning glory, and the $3/4$ inch that was left amounted to a "ruin." Never mind that the salon offered to pay another hairstylist to "attempt to correct the damage." It couldn't be corrected—there wasn't enough hair left.

Glenn's social life was a wreck. His friends made fun of him "because of the short hair on top of his head and the long hair on the sides." He took to wearing a cap. Finally, Glenn had to call a psychiatrist to treat his "panic anxiety disorder."

In short, Glenn told the judge, he had been "deprived of his right to enjoyment of life" and suffered "permanent and continuing" damages. Spare me, said the judge; it'll grow back. And he dismissed the case.

The Case of the Insulting Computer

Francis was working his way through a new computer program called "Learn to Type Right" when he came to a practice drill that gave him a jolt. It said: "Frankie says noxious things. He writes even worse. He tried to sell us some old junk. Nobody bought it; we wanted good help; sorry Frankie."

To Francis, whose nickname was Frank, this looked a lot like libel—from his very own computer program. He had written "Learn to Type Right." But he certainly hadn't written this paragraph. Francis fired off a letter of complaint to Sizzling Software Inc., the company that had paid him to create the program.

We'll take that part out of future editions, the company promised. And don't worry—no one would recognize "Frankie" as you anyway. (Apparently an unfriendly co-worker had stuck in the insult.)

Francis was not appeased. He was, as his lawyer pointed out, the only Frank in the credits. He sued Sizzling Software for $6 million. The company decided it didn't want to go to court for libel, and quietly settled the case.

The Case of the Dogged DEA Agent

On a tip, the police grabbed the luggage of Jason, a known drug runner, while he was held over in the airport. They called in the Drug Enforcement Administration.

Warren, the DEA agent, came running, but he didn't have a trained dog handy to sniff the suitcases. So he did the sniffing himself. Sure enough, Warren nosed out the odor of marijuana in two of the valises.

The police nabbed Jason and he was convicted. Jason, however, wasn't about to give in. I never got a chance to test Warren's sense of smell—no fair, he argued. On top of that, he added, the police destroyed the smell of marijuana when they opened the luggage—so the case ought to be dismissed on grounds of destruction of evidence!

Ridiculous, snorted the Appeals Court judge, and he threw Jason out of court. The sharp-nosed Warren, he found, "emerges with his nose unbloodied and his tail wagging."

The Case of the Gaseous Grocer

The two grocery store workers just couldn't seem to get along—you might say there was something in the air between them.

At least, that's what Jeff claimed when he got mad enough to take Marty to court. Jeff's complaint: Marty had "willfully and maliciously inflicted severe mental stress . . . by continually, intentionally, and repeatedly passing gas" in Jeff's direction.

Marty had a regular workday routine. He would "seek out" Jeff across the room, and then sidle up to him and take aim. Jeff put up with these salvos for just so long, then decided to fire one of his own. The U.S. courts might have seen $100,000 air-quality lawsuits before, but never one quite like this.

Jeff had some trouble finding a lawyer and finally decided to represent himself. The day of the big blowout arrived, and the courtroom was packed; word about this trial had leaked out. But the plaintiff apparently got cold feet—he never showed up in court.

At that, the judge dismissed the case. He probably would have done the same, Jeff or not. Marty's behavior may have been "juvenile and boorish," said the judge, but there didn't seem to be any law against it.

The Case of
the Disappearing Aura

Opal, a professional psychic, should have taken a peek at her own future before going to the hospital for some tests. The contrast dye used in the CAT-scan made me feel "as if my head was going to explode," Opal said, and what's more, the test made my psychic powers disappear!

Before the CAT-scan, Opal had been able to "read auras" around people, predict the future, and hold séances. More than once she had been a psychic mouthpiece for the poet John Milton. Opal not only advised private clients, but she also helped the police solve crimes and find missing persons.

But after the CAT-scan, Opal said, every time she tried to use her ESP, she got a splitting headache. Finally, she had no choice but to close her office, abandon her career, and call a lawyer.

I sympathize about the headaches, said the judge, but my sympathy only goes so far. He told the jury to make its award solely on the basis of Opal's pain at the time of the test—and to ignore the matter of her loss of powers.

The jury awarded her $600,000 anyway. With the added damages for delay (it was now ten years since the CAT-scan), her total came to almost $1 million. But riches were not in the cards for Opal: The judge's patience went up in a puff of smoke and he threw out the verdict.

The Case of the Dental Evangelist

Tune in a hell-bent preacher on TV and you can flip the channel. Meet him on a street corner and you can cross the street. But when the preacher has got you cornered in the dentist's chair—now, that's torture.

Loretta, a dental hygienist, had two callings: her job and her religion. Problem was, she insisted on combining the two. Just when she had her patient nicely trussed up with his mouth full of metal, Loretta would launch into a heartfelt spiel about her religious beliefs.

Bernard, the dentist she worked for, warned her again and again to quit "sharing her faith" this way. It got so that his patients wouldn't go anywhere near Loretta, and Bernard had to do the routine cleaning himself. Six patients left him altogether.

Finally, Bernard had no choice but to fire Loretta—and when she tried to collect unemployment insurance, the authorities said no. At this, Loretta cried foul. All she'd been doing, she said, was exercising her right to free speech.

But Loretta's prayers were lost on the court. She was "behaving against the best interests" of her boss, said the judge, and he was justified when he fired her. "A dentist has the right to expect his hygienist . . . not to add more discomfort to a patient's already uncomfortable situation."

III.
GOVERNMENT WASTE

The End of the Line

The General Services Administration spent $1.5 million—from a potential $13 million—to renovate an old, unused train station in Nashville, Tennessee. The only use the station got was as a home for a flock of roosting pigeons.

Beam Me Aboard, Scotty

What will the transportation needs of earthlings be in the year 2025? Well, the Department of Transportation spent $225,000 to find out. Some questions were formulated to include transportation needs in the United States if it is 1)transformed by an Ice Age, 2) taken over by a dictator, 3) dominated by a hippie culture.

Keep on Trucking

Have you ever considered these important questions: Do oversized trucks block your vision on the highway? Do they go up hills slowly? Do they contribute to traffic congestion? And do they make a big splash on wet roads? The Federal Highway Administration spent $220,000 to discover the astonishing answers. Their findings: You bet they do! We could have told the Federal Highway Adminstration that for a fraction of the price.

Jail Bait

The Law Enforcement Assistance Administration spent $27,000 on a study to determine why inmates escape from jail. The real crime was wasting $27,000 for the study.

Horsin' Around

The U.S. Air Force bestowed upon the University of Florida a $100,000 grant to see if the noise of low-flying F-4 Phantom fighter jets would have a negative effect on pregnant horses in the Southwest.

Bear Minimum

An employee of the U.S. Forest Service receives an annual salary in excess of $42,000 to oversee the trademark the government holds on Smokey the Bear.

Livin' High on the Hog

How should a pregnant pig be treated? And would she be less bored if she jogged? The U.S. Department of Agriculture (USDA) studied sows that were cooped up during pregnancy, and they noticed that all kinds of problems surfaced. The pigs suffered from tension and a lack of exercise. So, the USDA devised treadmills for them, to reduce the psychological stress on these mommies-to-be.

No More Monkey Business

Have you ever wondered why monkeys and rats clench their teeth? Well, the Office of Naval Research, the National Science Foundation, and the National Aeronautics and Space Administration found the answer. For $500,000 we now know that when monkeys and rats feel cheated, they get angry, scream, and kick, and clench their jaws.

Copyrats

Rats had a feast eating inside a $93,000 copy machine in the House Office Building. When the machine was opened up to find out why it wasn't working, an employee discovered that inside the copier were banana peels, corncobs, and a Hostess Twinkie still sealed in its plastic wrapping. With a $10,000 trade-in, a replacement machine cost the taxpayers an additional $97,000.

Amazing Alcohol

The National Institute on Alcohol Abuse and Alcoholism sponsored a project on aggressive behavior in fish after drinking alcohol. According to Dr. Harman Peeke, medical psychology professor at the University of California at San Francisco, fish were the only ethically acceptable subjects. It cost $102,000 to discover if sunfish that drink tequila are more aggressive than sunfish that drink gin.

How Sweet It Is

The National Aeronautics and Space Administration spent $200,000 to see if a sweet potato can be grown in outer space.

As Different as Apples and Oranges

How often have you heard combatants try to clarify their points of view by blurting out, "You're comparing apples to oranges." Well, the National Aeronautics and Space Administration (NASA) thought it was worth looking into this. NASA sponsored a team from Ames Research Center, Moffett Field, California, which compared Granny Smith Apples and Sunkist Navel Oranges. The team dried these fruits in a convection oven at a low temperature over the course of a few days. They then mixed these samples with potassium bromide and ground them in a mill. One hundred milligrams of the powders were thereafter pressed into a circular pellet. The findings? Apples and oranges are very similar. This should have a striking effect on future arguments and discussions.

What's Cooking at the Pentagon?

After a six month study, the Pentagon released its 22-page official brownie recipe. Here are some excerpts:

- The texture of the brownie shall be firm but not hard.
- Pour batter into a pan at a rate that will yield uncoated brownies which, when cut such as to meet the dimension requirements specified in regulation 3.4f, will weigh approximately 35 grams each.
- The dimensions of the coated brownie shall not exceed $3^1/2$" x $2^1/2$" x $^5/8$".
- Shelled walnut pieces shall be of the small piece size classification, shall be of a light color, and shall be U.S. No. 1 of the U.S. Standards for Shelled English Walnuts. A minimum of 90 percent, by weight, of the pieces shall pass through a $^4/16$-inch-diameter round hole screen and not more than 1 percent, by weight, shall pass through a $^2/16$-inch-diameter round-hole screen.

And here's what the Pentagon had to say about the proper pumpkin filling: "Good consistency means that the canned pumpkin . . . after emptying from the container to a dry-flat surface . . . holds high mound formation, and at the end of ten minutes after emptying on such surface, the highest point of the mound is not less than 60 percent of the height of the container."

Flying Potato Chips

The Aerochip Institute, Mountain View, California, conducted experiments to test this age-old adage: You can't throw a potato chip. Given that the aerodynamic properties of potato chips may depend on their size, shape, weight, etc., a number of different chip types were tested. The long-awaited results are:

- You can throw a potato chip, just not very far.
- The distance traveled is largely dependent on chip weight, shape, and freshness.
- Potato chips travel considerably farther when flying in formation, probably because such flight decreases the overall coefficient of drag.

Can't See the Forest for the Trees

The U.S. Forest Service was severely criticized for not hiring enough women as firefighters. The reasoning was that women weren't strong enough to lug the heavy firefighting equipment. When the EEOC got on its case, the Forest Service placed a job announcement stating that "Only unqualified applicants may apply." A second announcement stated that "Only applicants who do not meet [job requirement] standards will be considered."

PS: The Washington Times reported that many positions were not being filled because no qualified women were able to fill them.

Military Mania

Maine Senator William Cohen and Delaware Senator William Roth announced that the Navy was paying $640 for a toilet seat that would cost us only $25. And then there's the $400 hammer and $54 stapler.

Taken for a Ride . . .

The National Highway Traffic Safety Administration spent over $120,000 to test a back-wheel-steering motorcycle. Not surprisingly, it was impossible to steer.

Beep! Beep!

The National Science Foundation spent $46,000 to find out if distractions, such as sex, would decrease the honking of frustrated drivers stuck in traffic jams in cities. As bait, the agency hired bikini-clad women to roam the city streets. Instead of honking at these half-naked women, the men whistled and made lewd comments. Who would have expected . . .

The Lap of Luxury

Housing and Urban Development Secretary Samuel R. Pierce, Jr., won a Golden Fleece award for having the most expensive limousine of any cabinet member. He was one of 190 federal officials who received chauffeur services to their homes. This cost more than $3.4 million a year.

How Many Congress People Does It Take to Change a Light Bulb?

"All of them," according to Judd Rose of ABC News. At least, that was the case in Chambersburg, Pennsylvania. In 1991 Congress passed transportation legislation that dictated when traffic light bulbs could be changed. For example, in Chambersburg, bulbs could be changed between 8:00 and 8:30 am or 2:45 and 3:45 pm.

And that was one of hundreds of such projects governed by the law. It was also ordered that Chattahoochee, Florida, would get a bridge over Mosquito Creek. In New York, the Hellgate Viaduct would get a paint job. What's wrong with this, you may ask?

There was no need to put a bridge over Mosquito Creek and the Hellgate Viaduct didn't need painting.

The Ream Riddle

Q. How many pages does it take the Bureau of Land Management to request bids for fire equipment to be placed on two pickup trucks?

A. 125 pages of requirements and 23 foldout diagrams.

Runaway Spending

Fort Worth Regional Office of Urban Mass Transportation Administration (UMTA) received a Golden Fleece Award for this waste of money:

Two grants to help build bus garages to repair 150 and 200 buses, respectively. The problem with that was the fleets consisted of only 45 and 94 buses, respectively.

$1 million to replace trolley buses. The ridership at the time this was approved averaged fewer than two passengers per trip.

A Road Paved with Good Intentions

The Federal Highway Administration spent $21 million to pay for unused and unneeded roads and bridges. This is how it went:

- $900,000 for a four-lane bridge that had no road leading to or from it.
- 6.5 miles of new roadway, because traffic was supposed to double in 20 years. Somebody goofed because traffic declined by 50 percent.
- $26,000 for two extra-long overpass bridges because it was expected that the road underneath would be widened to four lanes. Twenty-five years after the money was invested, the road underneath remained two lanes.

Fasten Your Seat Belts

The government owns a fleet of more than 333,333 non-tactical vehicles (and that's not counting postal vehicles). If you add the price of the purchase of the cars, the chauffeurs and the overhead, we're spending about $150 million each year on our cruising congressionals.

Who Said There's No Such Thing as a Free Ride?

Taxpayers are spending almost $100 million each year to pay for the free subway rides of federal employees. In 1991 this bill was enacted by a Maryland senator and passed into law by President George Bush.

And speaking of free rides, more than $7 million is spent each year by politicians on junkets to popular vacation spots around the world. It's called "business travel." As a matter of fact, when the government's fiscal year is about to run out, there's an estimated 48 percent increase in government business travel.

Cookoo Choo-Choo

A recent issue of USA Today reported what is considered by some to be the biggest boondoggle in park history. Over a period of ten years, Rep. Joseph

M. McDade tapped taxpayers for $66 million to bail out rundown tourist attractions that went bankrupt after they have been removed from Vermont. (Why they were moved from Vermont in the first place wasn't mentioned.) One such boondoogle is the Steamtown National Historic Site Museum, which opened in Scranton, Pennsylvania. It's "not a monument to any critical event or location in railroad history, but a monument to the ability of Rep. Joseph M. McDade to play parochial politics," the newspaper reported.

The Friendliest Skies

If you wanted to take your family on a year-end vacation to Puerto Rico—that's if you can afford the vacation in the first place—wouldn't you try to find the airline that offers the best deal? But, if you're a cabinet official, there's no need to bother. The Special Airlift Mission (SAM) of the 89th Military Airlift Command will fly members of Congress first class and for free. All they have to do is call a few days in advance and a flight crew from Andrews Air Force Base will be assembled. The crew will order special cuts of beef and liquors. The cost? Over $8 million a year.

Spruce-Up Time

The U.S. Forest Service won the Golden Fleece Award for "Helistat," an experimental contraption under development in New Jersey. Four helicopters were yoked to a blimp for the purpose of lifting logs from remote corners of national forests. Dubbed "the mechanical mongrel" because it was riddled with cost overruns, construction foul-ups, and inadequate planning, "Helistat" cost $40 million.

Space-y Art

Anti-object artist Le Ann Wilchusky boarded a small aircraft armed with a large bundle of crepe-paper streamers. The plane took off, and at the appropriate moment, Ms. Wilchusky threw the streamers out into the sky. She later told reporters:

"I'm sculpting in space. A black streamer looks like a crack in the sky. Red and yellow streamers look like high lines, lashing the earth. By making people look upward, my work called attention to the higher spirit of mankind."

For this "higher spirit," the National Endowment for the Arts provided a $6,025 grant.

A Flying Leap

The Federal Aviation Administration (FAA) was the recipient of the Tenth-Anniversary Golden Fleece Award. The FAA received $48 million to enable municipal airports in Florida to use surplus federal land and buildings to help pay off their operating costs. At 23 of these airports, more than 9,000 acres are sitting idle because they're home to mosquitoes and sawgrass. The land has an estimated rental value of about $32 million per year. (Where are all of the realtors and developers when you need them?)

Clip Their Wings

The Department of Defense (DOD) spent $28,000 to shuttle nine members of Congress to Washington in a posh executive jet so they wouldn't miss a close vote on the MX missile. DOD lost the vote anyway—199 to 197—so the trip was not only illegal, but a waste of time. However, to demonstrate its gratitude to these congressional cruisers, the Department flew four of them back at a cost of $16,016. The same trip on a commercial airline would have cost $1,367.

Fly-by-Night Scheme

The National Oceanic and Atmospheric Administration established the Office of Aircraft Operations (OAO) to improve aircraft management. OAO bought two helicopters for $1.9 million to be used to improve safety in the Artic by exploring the Arctic Continental Shelf. The choppers are stationed in Miami.

From the Top Down

The FAA spent $57,800 on a head-to-foot physical study of 432 female flight attendants, involving 79 specific measurements. Such measurements included the popliteal length of the buttocks and the knee-to-knee breadth while sitting.

The Feeney Family

The FAA transferred traffic controller Brian Feeney, along with his wife and six children, to work in the San Juan, Puerto Rico radar center. The family was housed at the ESJ Towers Hotel overlooking the Caribbean. They stayed at the hotel for 90 days, which cost $32,400. In addition to that, the bill for their food for the first month alone was $12,419, even though their unit had complete kitchen facilities. When all the costs were added up, $77,000 was spent to feed and lodge the Feeney family for three months.

When Mrs. Feeney was questioned about these exorbitant expenses, she explained that the family ate out every night and spent about $200 for an average evening's meal. The guidelines set by the FAA allow $335 a day for food.

The Hutchins Family

Daniel Hutchins, his wife, and two very young daughters were transferred to the same center in San Juan. Their 90-day bill for food was $11,260.34. The family often at lunch at the Taco Maker, whose basic product is a 99-cent burrito. The restaurant owner estimated that an average meal for a family of four (and mind you, the two daughters were aged three and one) would cost about $15.48. Why did the FAA reimburse the family $130.15 per lunch at the Taco Maker?

Motivation by Disney

The Urban Mass Transit Administration sent its officials to Disneyworld in Orlando, Florida, to learn Disney's secrets of motivating employees. They discovered a new way to collect fares on "Space Mountain," an indoor roller-coaster-like ride. This junket cost $68,160.

Rats!

The National Institute on Alcohol Abuse and Alcoholism has also spent millions of dollars on experiments that turn rats into lushes.

And the Fish and Wildlife Service designated 77,000 acres in Riverside County, California, as a "rat preserve."

Does Census Make Sense?

The Comprehensive Employment and Training Act hired 101 people to go door-to-door to survey the number of dogs, cats, and horses in Ventura County, Virginia.

How Much Wood Could a Woodchuck Chuck if a Woodchuck Could Chuck Wood?

Once the experts at Harvard Medical School were able to repeat this tongue twister 100 times without making a mistake, they set out to get the answer. Twelve adult male woodchucks were volunteered for a two-week experiment. The experimenters defined "chuck" as 80 percent mastication and ingestion, 15 percent throwing wood around, and 5 percent vomiting.

Each "guest" was housed in a cage and deprived of all nourishment for one week. At the end of the seven days, each was fed through a pair of 5.08cm by 10.16cm holes in the sides of each cage. The animals were videotaped to see if they tried to:

• eat the 2 x 4 that was offered
• throw the 2 x 4 around the cage
• throw up

The findings were that all the hungry devils tried to eat the 2 x 4. (It is likely that most of the woodchucks, however, would have thrown the 2 x 4s at the observers, if given the chance.)

Stuffed Penguins

In 1994 scientists from the U.S. teamed up with scientists from New Zealand to find out why penguins in Antarctica are gaining weight. Every morning for three months the team would weigh 300 penguins immediately after they'd been fed. After the penguins regurgitated their food for their young, they'd be weighed again.

Wiggling Worms

The government funded a study at the University of Washington to monitor the defecation of worms. The scientists observed one-millimeter-long worms and a mutant strain they created. Both strains were constipated.

Barking up the Wrong Tree

The Department of the Interior spent $100,000 to train beagles to detect brow tree snakes in Hawaii. What's wrong with that? Tree snakes don't live in Hawaii; they're in Guam.

Grab the Bull by the Horns

"Bullfights and Ideology of the Nation in Spain" was the subject of a study done by the National Science Foundation to examine the dialectical relationship between the categories known as nations and regions in Spain, as they are manifested through the controversial spectacles known as bullfights. This bum steer cost $9,992!

Will Those Cockroaches Really Eat Anything?

The National Science Foundation gave $28,400 to a zoology professor to study the diet of desert cockroaches near Palm Springs, California.

Holy Cow!

The Environmental Protection Agency is giving Utah State University $500,000 to find out if belching cows contribute enough methane to affect global warming. The cows will be adorned with a special gizmo that will measure the volume of gas they release when they burp.

We've already paid for studies to determine the effect of cow emissions—gas at the other end—on global warming.

This Will Ruffle Your Feathers

The National Science Foundation is spending $155,358 for a three-year study to see if male blackbirds show off their wings to woo female blackbirds. Apparently, these "Romeo" birds spread and vibrate their feathers, and the researchers are not sure if this will get them something to chirp about.

Pigeon Economics

This relates to pigeons, but the study must have been authorized by cuckoos, because the government spent $144,000 to determine whether or not pigeons follow human economic laws.

A New Meaning to Bird Watching

The National Science Foundation and the National Institute of Mental Health sponsored a $107,000 study to understand the sexual behavior of the Japanese quail.

- the project was expected to "obtain evidence relevant to three sexual learning phenomena: sexual looking, classic conditioning of sexual arousal, and improvement of copulatory performance with practice."
- the project results were: when a sexually mature male was placed with a female, copulation occurred rapidly, often in less than five minutes, practice made perfect, as it did improve sexual performance, male quail spent a lot of time staring at female quail by peering through a small window in a nearby cage, and the "peeking" became such an event that the amorous males didn't care whether the objects of their desires were dead or alive.

Ouch! That Stings!

Now this is a honey of a deal. Beekeepers can get an interest-free government loan of 54 cents per pound of honey collateral. After the season, they have to repay only 49 cents. That's a 5-cent profit on the loan, no matter how good or bad a crop. This program costs over $100 million a year.

A Fly in the Ointment

The National Science Foundation has given $229,460 to scientists to study the sexual habits of 2,000 houseflies per week. The experiments will include creating transsexual male flies while blinding others and allowing them to mate through smell. The objective of this study isn't clear, but Gary Blomquist, the scientist heading the project, said: "We're looking at basic science here. I wouldn't even put a number on the years we need to study this. We're not even looking at control."

Where Does Charity Begin?

The Treasury Department has granted a $1.2 million tax loophole to U.S. citizens who live and work in foreign countries. This loophole allows them to exclude $70,000 of their income from their income tax. Proponents argue that this tax break is needed in order to reduce the trade deficit. They allege that Americans need tax incentives in order to work overseas and sell American-made products.

Lust for Knowledge

The National Institute of Mental Health (NIMH) granted Dr. Pierre van den Berghe, a full professor in the department of sociology and anthropology at the University of Washington in Seattle, $97,000 for prostitutes. Although it's not quite what you might think, ponder this.

The money was spent to study ethnic and class relationships among Indians and non-Indians in communities in the Andean village of San Tuti, Peru—a site outside of Cuzco. The study group? Prostitutes in Peruvian brothels. Prostitutes and madams were formally interviewed over the course of eighteen months. This was part of a larger study that focused on the nonsexual functions of the bordello as a male gathering place for drinking and storytelling and as an attraction for gringos.

To add insult to injury, the good professor submitted a brief report to NIMH and wrote a book on the subject. Even though the book was funded with tax dollars, he refused to give the agency a copy.

The Grand Pooh-Bah

Moroccan visitors, staying at the Watergate Hotel in Washington, ran up a tab of long-distance telephone charges totaling $499.68. The Moroccan Embassy told the Department of Defense (DOD) that if it wanted to collect, they'd have to go to Morocco. So, in its infinite wisdom, the DOD did. As taxpayers, we ended up spending $32,264.41 to recoup that $499.68.

The DOD also spent $15,532.50 for a Colombian

dignitary to visit Florida and then Washington, D.C. This funding included the rental of a yacht to have lunch on. The main menu item: filet de taxpayer.

We're Not Alone

If you think the United States has a monopoly on waste, think again! The government of Japan funded a seven-year study to determine whether earthquakes are caused by catfish wiggling their tails.

Parchment Paradise

The government has been studying the proliferation of paperwork and found that it spends in excess of $15 million a year on paper. It's one thing to do the study and another to do something about the study.

So, the Paper Management Office tried to encourage government employees to cut down on paperwork by having an annual contest. Letters (paper, of course) were sent out to government agencies telling them how to enter the names of nominees "who have contributed significantly to the efficiency or cost reduction of Federal paperwork systems." The nominating procedures were described in a six-page (paper) prospectus.

Decadent Decorating

For the modest sum of $325,000, the quarters of the "official temporary residence of the Vice-President of the United States" were refurbished. This breaks down as:

- $15,300 for china and crystal
- $18,100 for carpeting
- $21,200 for silverware
- $26,400 for drapes
- $33,000 for miscellaneous items
- $41,000 for furniture
- $170,000 for the replacement of window air conditioners with central air

Top-Secret Decorating

Nancy Reagan showed off her $1 million White House redecorating project to Architectural Digest, but forbade their letting the public see any of the photos.

All That Glitters

The Director of the Office of Management and Budget spent $611,623 to add gold trim to one medium-sized room in the Old Executive Office Building, which is next door to the White House.

Wired!

The Rural Electrification Administration (REA) was established to loan money to bring telephone service into rural areas. By the 1950s, however, 96 percent of the country had been wired, so the REA's job had been done. Instead of closing down shop, the REA started making loans to nuclear power plants that later went bankrupt. Now the money is going to:

- provide touchstone telephones to Micronesia
- run ski lifts in Vale and Aspen, Colorado
- electricity that powers golf carts in Hilton Head, South Carolina

No Business Like . . .

President Reagan said he wasn't fully informed about the Iran Arms deal—including an estimated $10 to $30 million that ultimately went to the opponents of the Sandinista government. He did have some good ideas about it, though, like when he called Ollie North to say, "This is going to make a great movie one day."

What about a Garage Sale?

The government spends between $250 million and $676 million on new furnishings each year. And this doesn't include expensive items, such as computer equipment.

Knock-Knock!
Anybody Home?

The National Reconnaissance Office is under construction near Dulles International Airport, in Virginia, with a price tag of $310 million. Just 30 miles away, members of the Senate Select Committee on Intelligence did not know the cost, though this intelligence group authorized the project and was "overseeing" it.

This Does Not Compute

The Department of Defense (DOD) purchased over $200 billion in computer equipment, which worked out like this:

The accounting department paid contractors $750 million in a six-month period. And the DOD was not able to define what goods and services they received for $41 million of that money.

The DOD's computerized inventory system bought $30 billion—yes, billion—of spare parts that proved unnecessary.

The military operates 161 major accounting systems, many of which are incompatible. So, the DOD relies on outside contractors to report when they're being overpaid.

Once the government buys computer equipment, it takes approximately 49 months (that's over four years) to install it. Since the computer industry is moving into a new generation of technology every 18 months, this means the government is continually buying outdated equipment. Private industry takes about one year to complete the purchase-to-installation cycle.

Mayor, Mayor on the Wall

The Minority Business Development Agency, a division of the Department of Commerce, awarded grants of $200,000 each year to the Lower Rio Grande Valley Conference of Mayors in southern Texas. After the first conference the Mayors deemed it useless and a waste of tax dollars. But the grants were renewed each year for four more years.

Another Government Gaffe

The Economic Development Administration, a division of the Department of Commerce, permitted local authorities to mismanage a federally funded revolving-door loan program. The program was intended to give grants to local areas to further economic development, increase incomes, and reduce unemployment. Instead, it hijacked jobs from one part of the country to another.

It cost $215 million.

Getting Something for Nothing

The Fish and Wildlife Service of the Department of the Interior mismanaged its payroll to the tune of $217 million. It continued to pay people who had left their jobs and granted overtime to people who were on vacation or away on personal leave.

Bookkeeping 101

The National Park Service, Division of the Department of the Interior, uses interesting accounting practices. It listed:

- a $350 dishwasher as a $700,000 asset
- a $150 vacuum cleaner as an $800,000 asset
- a fire truck as a one cent asset

I Should Get My Two Cents Out of This One

Resolution Trust Corporation recently hired Price Waterhouse to copy documents belonging to HomeFed Savings Association at the cost of 67 cents a copy. If you multiply that by the 10 million pages that were copied, the cost came to $6.7 million. Many copy shops charge 2 cents a copy.

Also, in 1992 when the Federal Deposit Insurance Corporation and Resolution Trust were asking Congress for more tax dollars, an audit revealed that these agencies had spent $3,098 for thirty-six coffee mugs and twelve T-shirts, and $1,800 for two breast pumps.

To Bee or Not to Bee

The United States government pays out more than $95 million a year in subsidies. To name only a few—very few—there's the National Soft Drink Association, the National Swimming Pool Association, the American Horse Council, the Tobacco Institute, as well as the Association of Beekeepers. By the way, beekeepers are not beekeepers, they are honey processors.

Several honey processors were at the Rayburn Congressional Office Building in Washington to educate Congress on the needs of honey people. Questions and answers went like this:

Q. What sort of help do you honey processors need?

A. Well, insecticide poisoning often kills our colonies and stops production.

Q. Aren't you reimbursed for that?

A. Uh . . . Yes, we are.

Q. Have you personally gotten money from the government?

A. Uh . . . Yes, on several occasions.

Q. How much did you get?

A. Uh . . .

Q. How much did you get?

A. Uh . . .

Q. Okay, roughly how much did you get?

A. Roughly $500,000.

Florida Fiascos

What would be a better winter weekend for politicians than one spent in Florida—away from the punishing storms and brutal temperatures much of the country is experiencing—courtesy of lobbying groups, such as U.S. Tobacco and the insurance lobbyists. And it's not only the politicians who are getting the red carpet treatment. Lobbyists are so aimed at building relationships that they wine and dine not only congressional staffers, but also young administrative assistants.

ABC News cameras followed our congressional teams on such a trip to Florida's Gold Coast. The group was entertained at an exclusive Boca Raton resort and club. In one weekend, the tab was more than $150,000. Tennis pros, such as Ilie Nastasi and Roscoe Tanner, were brought in to play with the lawmakers.

Federal Frequent Flyer: And the Winner Is . . .

John B. Breaux, Democratic Senator from Louisiana, has been on the congressional travel circuit. Lobbyists have paid for his trips to West Palm Beach, Fort Myers, Fort Walton Beach, Scottsdale, Palm Springs, Las Vegas, San Diego, and San Francisco. In his own defense, Senator Breaux said, "I don't select where they [the lobbyists] have conferences, they do."

Orange Diplomas

The U.S. Naval Academy suffered from weeks of altercations. Members of the 1990 graduating class had cheated on exams and chained coeds to urinals as part of a hazing process. So, when they graduated, the Academy awarded them diplomas from the U.S. Navel Academy. (A proofreading gaffe, of course!)

More Padding Than a Cushioned Toilet Seat

Remember when Maine Senator William Cohen and Delaware Senator William Roth announced that the Navy was paying $640 for a toilet seat that would cost us only $25? $400 for a hammer? $54 for a stapler, $50 of which is for paperwork.

Well, the National Aeronautics and Space Administration spent $23 million to build a prototype toilet for the space shuttle. The price tag represented a 900 percent increase over the original estimate, because the astronauts requested a manual flush rather than an automatic one.

How about Footing This Bill?

The United States Navy spent $792 for a designer doormat. The Navy is supposed to protect our seas so the enemy doesn't reach our doorstep, but this is going too far.

Spark Plugs

The U.S. Navy announced to the House Armed Services Oversight and Investigations Committee that it was paying $544.09 for a spark plug connector that could be bought off the shelf at hardware stores for $10.99. Adding sparks to this fire, the $544.09 connector required a five-month delivery period.

More Power to You

The Navy allotted $11.5 million to modernize the power plant at the Philadelphia Naval Yard. The plant had been scheduled to close.

This Is No Beach Party

The United States Navy wanted to improve its ship-to-ship communications, so it experimented with Frisbees to send messages. We haven't heard the dollar amount that was tossed away.

No More Bull

The Navy spent $10,000 on a study to determine the effect of naval communications on the potency of a bull.

Out on a Limb

The Department of the Army decided to use its surplus money to spruce up Fort Belvoir, Virginia, by planting decorative trees. The trees and shrubs died within a year and had to be uprooted. The landscape design cost $35,000 and the trees cost $124,000. We do not know the uprooting cost.

Making a Mountain Out of a Molehill

Have you ever played the game called "King of the Hill?" Each player strives to climb to the top of a hill and prevent all the other players from pushing him/her off. Well, the U.S. Army spent $20,000 to produce 30,000 pamphlets explaining this game. The pamphlet contained:

- a preface
- four pages of detailed rules
- a multicolored diagram of an earthen mound

Multiple Choice

Since 1946 the U.S. Army School of the Americas at Fort Benning, Georgia, has trained more than 56,000 Latin American soldiers. Among its graduates, whose educations were funded, include:

- Manuel Noriega, Class of 1972: voted "most likely to succeed"
- Roberto d'Aubuisson, Class of 1972: Managed Salvadorian death squads and ordered the assassination of a Catholic bishop while conducting Mass.

Since 1991, as a result of the atrocities of these grads, the school has mandated that students participate in a four-hour program on human rights. Here is one of the questions the students must answer:

Scenario: The squad leader gives an order to cut off the ears of dead enemy soldiers as proof of the number of casualties. You should:

a. Obey the order but denounce it to your superiors.

b. Obey the order.

c. Disobey the order and tell your superiors.

d. Order a squad member of lower rank to obey the order.

No News Might Be Good News

The Pentagon spends $162 million a year to produce and buy periodicals and newspapers, though it admits that most of them are nonessential and that many are repetitious. The Department of Defense spends $20.4 million for much of the same stuff. Each branch of the military, being a separate entity, wants its own publications.

Lottery Anyone?

In 1989 Congress authorized the Pentagon to spend $49,000 to determine if members of the armed forces would buy military lottery tickets.

Barely Acceptable

The taxpayers paid the salary of a senior Naval officer who had female Navy civilian employees pose nude for photographs. He claimed the photographs would be used for a series of training posters on board ships that were deployed to the Persian Gulf during the Gulf War. The shots were a cleaning sequence that started with routine deck scrubbing to wet T-shirts to more revealing poses. A favorite of many wives who posed was a "housecleaning, laundry, kitchen work sequence designed to emphasize their hard work at home." The good news is that the captain was charged with conduct unbecoming an officer. He was fined $1,000 and asked to resign.

Tell It to the Tooth Fairy

The Pentagon spent $2,000 to bury the tooth of Army Warrant Officer Gregory S. Crandall at Arlington National Cemetery. Crandall's dog tags had been found in 1971, and it was assumed that his helicopter crashed in Laos. The tooth was buried in a full-sized casket with full military honors. Crandall's family was appalled and attended under protest. The family sent out announcements that read: "The family of Warrant Officer Gregory S. Crandall regrets to announce the burial of a single tooth as his remains at Arlington National Cemetery on September 17 at 1:00. Your attendance is welcome."

No 20/20 Vision

Using the code name "Star Gate," the Pentagon has spent more than $20 million to employ psychics to pursue the unknown. The Pentagon hoped these crystal-ball gazers would give the Defense Intelligence Agency a paranormal advantage. According to David Goslin of the American Institute for Research, "There's no documented evidence that it [the psychic program] had any value to the intelligence community." For example, in 1981, when an American general, James Dozier was kidnapped, one psychic told the Pentagon that he was being held in Italy, in a stone house with a red roof. Well, that accounts for most Italian homes!

Family Feud

Don't we have anything better to do since the Cold War ended? We spent $150,000 to study the feud between the Hatfields and the McCoys.

Just the Fax, Ma'am

The Air Force spent $94.6 million to buy 173 fax machines designed by Litton Industries. These fax machines cost $547,000 each but will survive nuclear blasts. Senator Carl Levin, Democrat from Michigan, found out that the Air Force had rejected fax machines built by Magnavox that cost only $15,000 each.

Tools of the Trade

Pratt & Whitney told the Air Force it needed pliers to modify engines on F-111 aircraft. The contractor hired a subcontractor to build the pliers for $669 each. The subcontractor then added in $330.20 in overhead and profit. Thus, each pair of pliers cost $999.20.

Quail Cuisine

The government spent $22,000 and used military aircraft to fly two Air Force officials to Washington, DC, for a quail breakfast. It was a purely social engagement.

Soaring with Eagles and Trucking with Turkeys

A month before Thanksgiving in 1993, the Department of Agriculture launched unannounced inspections of turkey processing plants and issued the results after Thanksgiving. "If you're going to put out warnings or tell the results of the inspection," reasoned Representative John Mica, Republican from Florida, "wouldn't it be wise to do it prior to the season when you have the highest consumption?"

Money Down the Drain

Over $1 million was given to Trenton, New Jersey, for a sewer line so it could bypass a 100-year-old sewer that had been declared a landmark. This historic landmark is a brick lined sewer that's 25 feet underground. It has been visited by only two people in 23 years.

This Is a Backhanded Shot

The National Endowment for the Arts spent $2,500 to find out why people are rude and ill-mannered on the tennis court. The outcome of this study is unknown, but it won its approval in Faquier and Rappahannock counties, Virginia. Its purpose was to solve the problem of people having to wait hours for court time, and getting them to understand that there wasn't enough money in local budgets to build additional courts. The recipient of this Golden Fleece Award, Helen Sweeney, director of Arlington's Williamsburg recreation district, said about the award: "I'm perplexed, but I'm enjoying it."

The Wave of the Future?

"Federal Bureaucrats Make Waves and the Taxpayer Gets Soaked." This headline ushered in an historic moment. The Bureau of Outdoor Recreation of the Department of the Interior spent $145,000 to install a surf-making machine in a double-Olympic sized swimming pool in Salt Lake City. The rationale? A spokesman for the project claimed that "Residents will no longer need to jump in their campers and travel 300 miles to feel the rushing water of Flaming Gorge."

Up the Creek without a Paddle

The Bureau of Housing and Urban Development bestowed over $1 million on Pittsburgh, Pennsylvania, for building as access road, ramp, and tunnel to a private entertainment spa. This was to include sightseeing and shuttle boats, and a three-tiered floating dock. What's so odd about that?

• The passenger boat ended up in New York.
• The whereabouts of the shuttle is unknown.
• The dock emerged as two barges.

Sandbagging Us All?

Imagine the U.S. Army Corps of Engineers spending $33 million to pump sand onto ten miles of beach in Miami, Florida. This will probably add to the pleasures of those who stay in the condominiums and hotels. But geologists expect that Miami Beach will eventually become the Miami seawall. The Corps has talked about starting work on another 2.5 miles because "local interests desire extension to the northern limit." What's the limit? Palm Beach? Virginia Beach? Bar Harbor?

The Joker's Wild

The Department of the Air Force spent $59,000 for decks of cards that were given as souvenirs to visitors aboard Air Force Two. (Does it make you wonder if the Executive Office is playing with a full deck?)

This Is a Bat-ty One

Imagine spending $100,000 to construct a 100-foot baseball bat. The Works Progress Administration didn't just imagine it—they did it! If anyone finds a use for this bat, please let me know.

Absolutely Wreck-reational

Are rock concerts, golf balls, and health club memberships vital to our national security? Well, auditors for the Department of Defense have blown the whistle on Martin Marietta and its subsidiaries for charging the government:

- $263,000 for a Smokey Robinson concert in Denver, Colorado
- $20,194 for professional-quality golf balls
- $17, 487 for softball and volleyball games.

Another unnamed contractor submitted a bill for $144,000 for health club memberships and $55,000 for tea and coffee.

Return to Sender

Over $137,000 of our tax dollars sent 85 postal executives to a tennis resort south of Orlando, Florida. The intent was to prepare them for improved delivery of the Christmas mail. The curriculum included classroom and outdoor training on 30-foot poles and rope ladders designed to give obstinate managers a "breakthrough experience."

It Pays to Advertise

Can U.S. Savings Bonds be sold in the same way as bras and automobiles? The answers is probably yes, because the Federal government was ranked 28th by the magazine Advertising Age on its annual list of the nation's 100 leading advertisers. In one year alone, the government gave almost $229 million to the admen. In that same year Proctor & Gamble spent almost $774 million and Sears spent $732.5 million.

'Ad' This to the List

As part of its "Market Promotion Program," Uncle Sam picks up the tab for billions of advertising dollars. Our Uncle surely has his favorite nieces and nephews:
- $5.1 million was given to Gallo Wines.
- Tyson Chickens received $1.1 million.
- Ocean Spray was the beneficiary of $1 million.

- $6.2 million was given to Blue Diamond Almonds.
- McDonald's received $465,000.

We're also picking up the tab for over $70 million given to Sunkist to help them advertise overseas the oranges we're not allowed to buy in the United States.

Beauty Is Only Skin Deep

However, it digs deep into our pockets, too. Look at what it cost to renovate the House Beauty Salon—$350,000.

Keep Those Cards and Letters Rollin'

The U.S. Postal Service spent $3.4 million on a Madison Avenue ad campaign to persuade us to write more letters. A spokesperson for the Postal Service claimed that its purpose was to increase the volume of mail. Low volume is one of the causes of the agency's chronic deficit. Then they spent $775,000 more to see if the campaign was working. The answer hasn't been disclosed.

Winning Losses

In 1993 the Post Office lost $500 million, which was $215 million over the losses that were expected. Shortly thereafter, Postmaster General

Marvin Runyon announced large cash bonuses for his top managers if they could keep the losses to $1.3 million. Are we paying bonuses for losses?

No-go Logo

Also in 1993, while the Post Office laid off 30,000 workers in an effort to cut costs, it spent $7 million to replace its logo. Runyon justified this expense by saying that it represented a "clean break with our bureaucratic past."

Indoor Plumbing

The manager of a Chicago post office exercised "poor judgment," according to officials, when she spent $200,000 to have a bathroom and kitchen renovated. Prior to the time the renovation started, the post office was slated to move to a new site one block away.

Who Said There's No Free Parking?

The Treasury Postal Service spent $2.4 million for the construction of a parking lot that would provide 200 parking spaces for federal employees. There were only 18 federal employees in the facility.

No Reverence

The son of John Zwynenburg was one of the tragic victims of Pan Am Flight 103 in 1988. The Internal Revenue Service guesstimated that the Zwynenburg family would be awarded over $11 million for their son's death and gave the bereaved family 90 days to pay taxes on that amount of money, even though no settlement had been reached.

Under Protest

Brooklyn retiree John McCormick sent a check to the Internal Revenue Service (IRS) with his tax return. Underneath his signature he wrote the words "under protest." The IRS slapped him with a penalty of $500. There were no inaccuracies in his return; this was a flagrant fine. Mr. McCormick went to court because the First Amendment of the Constitution "protects the right of protest to any branch of government." Apparently this doesn't apply to the IRS, because the judge ruled against this retiree.

IRS Compensation

In 1992 the Internal Revenue Service overpaid $20 billion in Earned Income Tax Credit to people who hadn't even applied. This program was designed to help workers poor enough for welfare, but 90 percent of the benefit checks went to people like illegal aliens and prisoners who have no income at all.

Murphy's Law of Computers

The IRS was trying to collect $2 million in back taxes from Joseph H. Hale, who was serving time in a federal prison. Instead, the IRS issued him a check for $359,380.25. Two years later the IRS had recovered $55,558.34 of the money. It seemed that Hale had a friend who helped him dispose of the rest.

'Why Do Fools Fall in Love?'

This "love story" was the recipient of the first Golden Fleece Award. The National Science Institute wanted to find out why and for how long males and females are attracted to each other. The cost of this fiscal fling? $84,000.

A Sense of Community

Once upon a time in a small community near Merrill Township, Michigan, the Bureau of Housing and Urban Development (HUD) approved $279,000 to build a community center for counseling, distributing food stamps, and conducting literacy classes and job training. The site selected was secluded in a virtually inaccessible forest.

Funds were not sufficient to complete a road to the site, so a partial road was built that did not reach anywhere near the community center. The road extended far enough to permit walkers to get to a narrow path, which ended in a pile of rubble. Without a road leading to the center, the project literally collapsed, but HUD never even knew it. So, there sits an inaccessible, unused community center built in the middle of nowhere.

'I Do' or 'I Don't'

Spent by the National Science Foundation to study the role of non-marriage in rural Irish families: $28,578. Apparently, Ireland has one of the highest rates of late and non-marriage.

Utter Nun-Sense

The National Institute of Health spent over $1 million to explore the incidents of cervical cancer in women. For this study, two groups of women were used: nuns who are virgins and "nuns who are sexually active."

'X' Marks the Spot

The National Institute of Neurological and Communicative Disorders and Stroke conducted a study to determine whether someone can place a hex on an opponent during a strength endurance test by drawing an "X" on the front of the opponent's chest. What a boon this could be for the 98-pound weakling! The Institute tried to justify this $160,000 expense with the following statement:

"The phenomenon under investigation cannot be understood or explained by information currently available and it is of obvious interest to determine what other heretofore unknown factors or mechanisms significantly influence muscle strength and movement."

All Washed Up

In 1993 the Environmental Protection Agency initiated a study into the hazards of breathing while taking a shower. They were specifically interested in seeing whether a person might be harmed by inhaling water vapor.

Can You Say, "Oxymoron?"

The Centers for Disease Control and Prevention (CDCP) spent $1,015,900 on a posh gathering of 238 employees at the Century Plaza Hotel in Beverly Hills, California, to discuss problems involved in vaccinating low-income children. House Health and Environmental Subcommittee Chairman Scott Klug, Democrat from Wisconsin, estimated that the amount of money spent on these employees could have immunized 13,500 children.

A Hare-Raising Experience

In 1993 the Physician's Committee for Responsible Medicine spent $3 million to determine if marijuana could make rabbits more prone to syphilis and mice more prone to Legionnaire's disease.

Use It or Lose It

When $122 million was allocated for an addition to the Dirksen Office Building in Washington, DC, it went to give the senators a third gymnasium.

Boob Tube

The Department of Education spent $219,000 to teach college students how to watch television effectively.

Send a Lawyer to Camp?

Should doctors, lawyers, and school administrators get away for free summer vacations? Free summer vacations? The National Endowment for the Humanities feels it's imperative "to broaden and sharpen their perspectives."

Lowdown Louisiana

Another Golden Fleece Award winner . . . According to an audit prepared by the Inspector General of the Department of Education, DOE fleeced the taxpayers for $912,678 by allowing education officials in Louisiana to divert money earmarked for handicapped children. Instead of providing for the needs of these children, $385,200 was spent on computer projects for the general student population. Inexperienced and noncertified personnel approved this three-year-long ripoff and paid for a staff person to work nine months, when in fact the person only worked six weeks.

My Oh Mayan

Do you speak Tzotzil? Do you know people who speak Tzotil? If you answer yes to either of these questions, perhaps you can figure out how the Smithsonian Institution can justify spending $89,000 to produce a Tzotil dictionary.

About 120,000 Mayan descendants, peasants in a corn-farming town in southern Mexico, speak Tzotil, an unwritten—yes, unwritten—language.

Research Grants

Universities receive billions of dollars each year to conduct research. But how far does research extend? Let's examine the research of Stanford University. It spent:

- $7,000 for sheets to cover the enlarged bed of the dean.
- $1,000 a month to wash the dean's laundry
- $1,500 for liquor for pre-football games, parties, etc.

Other universities, such as Rutgers, Yale, Duke,

Emory, Johns Hopkins, and MIT, were earmarking funds for trips to Europe and the Caribbean, artwork, foreign language lessons, storytelling for Christmas functions, sabbaticals, and golf club memberships—all in the name of learning.

All in the Name of Learning

The following universities billed the government for these expenses:
- Dartmouth College—$20,490 to chauffeur the president of the college and his wife
- Massachusetts Institute of Technology—$4,655 for its contribution to the Museum of Fine Arts
- Cornell University—$1,000 for a Steuben glass wine goblet
- Stanford University—$3,000 for a cedar-lined closet, and $2,000 for monthly deliveries of flowers to the home of the university president.

Rock 'n' Roll

The National Institute of Education spent $900,000 to buy a disco and promote a rock concert.

Here's Egg in Your Face

The United States Department of Agriculture performed a study to see how long it takes to fry eggs in a skillet. After spending $46,000 we know it takes 838 time measurement units (TMUs).

Down on the Farm

The Environmental Protection Agency spent over $38,000 to determine if the runoff from open stacks of cow manure on farms in Vermont was causing pollution in water in nearby streams and ponds.

Bamboo-zelled

The Department of Agriculture spent $63,000 on bamboo research. None grows in the U.S.

How Long Can It Last?

This can only happen in the federal fertilizer factory, which is the National Fertilizer Development Center in Muscle Shoals, Alabama. During World War II, the plant was designed to produce nitrate to be used in munitions. The government no longer needs the fertilizer, but it still donates $20 million a year to this plant.

The Connecticut Con

Would you consider Fairfield County, Connecticut, one of the wealthiest suburbs of New York City, to be a farm in need of government aid? Back in the 1930s it was, but not anymore. This area, however, still has farm status according the Department of Agriculture (DOA). Therefore, the Oxbridge Hunt

Club, where it costs $20,000 to board your horse, was given money by the DOA to help build a dock to haul off their manure.

This Is a Meaty One

The Department of Agriculture spent $90,000 to study the "behavioral determinants of vegetarianism."

Playground of the Rich and Famous

The Bureau of Housing and Urban Development has also placed welfare families on the expensive island of Nantucket, Massachusetts. HUD is paying in the neighborhood of $1,750 a month for apartments to house these folks.

In the Lap of Luxury

You may not be rich enough to live next door to Hollywood celebs, but you certainly may be poor enough.

Housing and Urban Development is spending about $8 million to house 28 welfare families in the middle of one of California's most expensive seaside neighborhoods. The "La Jolla Villas" will offer subsidized rents starting at $323 a month in an area where a mid-priced home can go for a half million. In addition to an ocean view, each welfare family will also have its dues paid for the local country club. This tab is $310 per month per family, for an additional $104, 160.

Mel Shapiro, local housing rights activist, values this land at $2.5 million. He expressed his disgust when he said, "I'm a housing advocate, not an idiot."

What's the Resale Value?

In 1986 the National Park Service bought a half acre of land in southwest Washington, DC, for the price of $230,000. Two years later a search showed that the National Park Service had already owned the land. It had purchased that same parcel in 1914.

Icy Finding

What was the climate like in Africa during the last Ice Age? Cold. It took $121,000 of our tax dollars to find that out.

Someone Should Be WIPP-ed for This

The U.S. Department of Energy has dug a big hole in the ground called the Waste Isolation Pilot Plan (WIPP). It was supposed to be America's trash dump for low-level, non-toxic waste. This seven-mile tunnel, which stretches a half mile underground, was finished in 1989. But with changing regulations and lawsuits, it still hasn't opened.

Meanwhile, it costs more than $7 million a year to maintain it. That brings the cost to more than $2 billion, since the project started in the 70's. Even though WIPP isn't opened, it employs:

- 45 people to keep nuclear records (There are no records to keep.)
- elevator operators (Who's being lifted and lowered?)
- guards (What are they guarding? Their lunch?)
- a public relations staff of over 2,000 (It sounds more like private relations, not public.)

WIPP has been criticized by its own proponents, who claim that with better management the government could have saved the taxpayers more than $400 million from 1989 to 1994. If the plant is to open, another $1.5 million needs to be poured into the hole.

Operating in the Hole

The Department of Labor's Mine Safety and Health Administration (MSHA) is supposed to recover the entire cost of equipment testing by passing the charges along to the manufacturer of the equipment. But it seems MSHA didn't charge the manufacturers enough. The expenses to the taxpayers mounted to a $10 million tab.

More Waste (Literally)

In Yucca Mountain, Nevada, the Department of Energy (DOE) wanted to store the nation's nuclear waste and decided to build a repository for that purpose. In order to dig the tunnel, DOE bought a 25-foot tunnel-boring machine that cost $13 million. The government already owned an 18-foot boring machine that would have been more than adequate to dig the tunnel.

DOE was advised by its technical review board that if it bought the bigger machine, it would have to buy a special conveyor belt that would cost another $2.25 million. So, DOE is back on Capitol Hill asking for the additional $2.25 million, while the 25-foot tunnel-boring machine is tunneling along, slowly and inefficiently.

IV.
COURTROOM ANTICS

Wheeling and Dealing

The Americans with Disabilities Act forced the owner of the Odd Ball Cabaret—a Los Angeles strip joint—to close because the dancing stall on the stage wasn't accessible to a stripper in a wheelchair.

Guilty When Proven Innocent

Federal agents can use your tax dollars to seize your home, wallet, car, and other possessions, even if you are completely innocent of any crime. If you want to get your property back, you have to post a bond equal to 10 percent of the value of your property. This is to cover the government's costs in defending itself against you. And it can cost you tens of thousands of dollars in your own legal fees to recoup your possessions.

Anonymous Call

In East Hartland, Connecticut, agents seized the home of Walter and Joann Cwikla because they had received an anonymous call that the Cwiklas were storing a small amount of marijuana. Federal agents never even searched the home; they merely confiscated it and nailed a notice on the front door declaring that the property had been seized. After five years and $25,000 in legal fees, this couple is still trying to reclaim their home.

Gray Druggies

In 1991, agents raided the Utah home of an elderly couple named Robert and Vera Garcia. The agents confiscated their home, their retirement savings, and a few hundred dollars in cash. The agents claimed that all the Garcias' possessions were purchased with drug money. No evidence was ever found to substantiate this, and the agents have offered no evidence to justify that seizure. However, the Garcias have had none of their property returned.

To the Victor . . .

Here are two of countless examples showing how confiscated assets are being spent:
- Officers in Greensboro, North Carolina, used seized loot to pay for equipment for an exercise room for themselves.
- In Erie County, New York, confiscated money was used by the sheriff to buy himself a snappy red Ford Crown Victoria car. A similar purchase was made in Suffolk County, New York—only that agent bought a BMW.

Order in the Court

An Iowa woman was accused of stealing a $25 sweater. Shortly thereafter, agents confiscated her $18,000 car that was specifically equipped to transport her disabled daughter. They claimed the vehicle was used as the getaway car.

A judge in Worcester, Massachusetts, responded to the plea of a thief claiming he stole while under hypnosis. The judge advised the defendant to get re-hypnotized so he wouldn't mind spending 10 years in jail.

Bert Winkler, of Yazoo City, Mississippi, was brought to trial on charges of bank robbery. He convinced a friend to slip the jurors a note saying he'd give them each $1,000 if they acquitted him. After he was found not guilty, Winkler gave each juror $1,000, the judge $5,000, and the bailiff $250. He even gave $5 to each person who attended the trial, and gave the prosecuting attorney a nickel.

A woman in Norfolk, Nebraska, was brought to court for crossing the street against a red light. For this infraction, she was fined $2.50. The woman gave the clerk a $5 bill and turned around to leave before receiving her change. When the judge called after her, she turned around and said, "That's okay, I need to cross back to the other side."

A woman in Haleiwa, Hawaii, was stopped on Highway 83 by a police officer for going 65 mph in a 45 mph zone. She appealed the case and told the judge she was rushing home because she had to take her birth control pill "before it's too late." The judge admitted the originality of her allegation, but fined her anyway.

Inane Insurance Claims

These were taken from reports that policyholders were asked to fill out following automobile accidents:

- The pedestrian had no idea which direction to go, so I ran over him.
- Coming home, I drove into the wrong house and collided with a tree I didn't have.
- The accident happened when the right front door of a car came around the corner without giving a signal.
- The telephone pole was approaching fast. I was attempting to swerve out of its path when it struck my front end.
- I was on the way to the doctor's with rear-end trouble when my universal joint gave way causing me to have an accident.
- The guy was all over the road. I had to swerve a couple of times before I hit him.

And Baby Makes Three

In Kampuchea, a hamlet of Paoy Pet, children outnumber adults five to one. The voting age is seven, and the mayor is only nine. Because children rule, they can punish their parents if they've been bad.

The six-year-old son of the mayor in Tadmor, Syria, was kidnapped by terrorists. The mayor refused to pay ransom, claiming that his son was always misbehaving. The boy behaved so badly, the terrorists returned him for the equivalent of $.50 and the mayor's promise not to prosecute.

The Bear Facts

The Department of the Interior was responsible for passing the Endangered Species Act. As a result, a Montana rancher named John Shuler was stiffly fined for shooting a bear that attacked him on his own land. Grizzly bears had been mauling Shuler's sheep for months. One night he heard a disturbance; he grabbed his gun and ran outside. He saw four grizzlies. Three were attacking his sheep and one was running toward him. Shuler shot the bear and ran back to his home for safety. The judge fined him $4000, declaring him at fault because "he purposefully placed himself in the zone of imminent danger."

Playing Chicken

In Kankakee, Illinois, a woman brought charges against a masher because he called her a chicken. The judge asked the woman how much she weighed, calculated what she would cost per pound if she were a chicken, and fixed that sum as the masher's fine.

It's a Dog's Life

In South Bend, Indiana, Brutus was put on trial. Brutus was a guide dog who walked his masters into walls, pulled them down flights of stairs, and walked them into manholes. Brutus had three owners and he was finally brought to court and found guilty of manslaughter. Brutus was sentenced to death.

Pearl-y Words

A man and woman were dining at a restaurant in Scranton, Pennsylvania. The woman ordered an oyster dish. The oyster contained a pearl that was valued at $750. Both the woman and the restaurant owner claimed they owned the pearl, and the case went to court. The judge, in his attempt to make an impartial ruling, awarded the pearl to the gentleman who paid for the woman's dinner.

Stinky Stuff

A woman in Jonesboro, Arkansas, was arrested for selling onions on Sunday; she was in violation of the local blue laws. The judge concluded that the woman was innocent because "an onion can sometimes take the place of a fruit, especially as dessert."

Talking Teeth

Chicago Tribune columnist Mike Royko reported that charges were brought by the Americans with

Disabilities Act against a private company because the company refused to hire a man who professed to have a microchip in one of his teeth. He claimed the microchip allowed him to communicate with people far, far away.

No More Pink Slips

In a 1994 speech, EEOC lawyer Davie Fram inferred that companies must exercise extreme caution when they discipline employees who attack their supervisors, because the employee may have a mental disability that the company must accommodate.

What ForeSIGHT!

The Federal Highway Administration proposed a bill so that truck drivers who were blind in one eye and had poor vision in the other could get driver's licenses. (Fortunately a judge had the fore "sight" to see the perils of this bill and shot it down.)

It's What's Up Front That Counts

The U.S. Bureau of Alcohol, Tobacco, and Firearms (BATF) recently banned one brand of Italian wine, Collio, because the bottles displayed bosomy naked women. So Collio began shipping bottles with flat-chested naked women, and BATF did not object. Dot Koester, spokesperson for the agency, said, "There is nothing objectionable about being perfectly flat-chested. The label is like seeing a man at the beach."

Supervigilant!

The Food and Drug Administration (FDA) might be going a bit far. It has been trying to govern the distribution of sunglasses and frames, a wheelchair cushion, a dental bib, a low-pressure mattress, and a foot comforter massage.

Sign on the Dotted Line

The Food and Drug Administration (FDA) has refused to approve a pump that can save the life of heart attack victims. This device has been so successful in Austria and France that it is mandatory equipment on ambulances in those two countries. Why is the FDA refusing? The agency insists that the pump makers get the "informed consent" of any patient on whom the pump is tested. That's not very likely to happen, because at the point that this pump would be effective, the victims are clinically dead.

Legal Eagles

A Minnesota tax form asked for all sorts of information. It requested that you fill in your date of birth and your date of death.

This Seat's Taken

The EEOC deemed that obesity is protected under the Americans with Disabilities Act of 1990. Southwest Airlines was sued by a 400-pound woman when an agent allegedly asked the woman to purchase two seats.

V.
WHAT'S THE VERDICT:
Test Your Legal Knowledge

The following are real court cases taken from published reports. The cases come primarily from the United States. A few are from the United Kingdom and Canada. Most of the cases date from the last half of this century, although several are more than a hundred years old.

All the cases were the subjects of appeal to a higher court. This indicates that the point of law involved is difficult and caused reasonable jurists to disagree over the result. On appeal, many of the judgments were not unanimous; this further shows that the legal issues are not easy.

In addition, the cases are consistent with the general current of the law in the United States and in common law countries. This does not mean that a court hearing a particular case today would necessarily decide the case in the same way that it was decided before. It does mean, however, that the analysis of the court would proceed along the same lines and consider generally the same arguments. Having stated this qualification, we nevertheless believe that the vast majority of the cases in this book would probably be decided the same way today as they were when they were tried.

Throughout, the authors have also striven for uniformity of philosophy and approach. In other words, the results in the cases are not arbitrary. No decision in this section directly contradicts another. No reader will be frustrated because of lack of internal consistency within this section.

We have also made every attempt to avoid trick solutions to the cases. There are no rabbits pulled out of hats. Where we thought a legal principle was needed to decide a case, we summarized that principle for the reader.

Facts are always crucial to the resolution of a legal dispute. All the facts that you will need are laid out in the synopsis of the case. Don't be tempted to add new facts or to embellish existing ones. You will not be asked to decide, for example, whether a particular individual is telling the truth or not in a particular case. You can safely assume the truth of the facts and the assertions in the cases, unless you are asked to do otherwise in the question itself.

You, the reader, are actually being asked to do a dual job. First, you play the role of the jury. You are not expected to decide the facts, but rather to apply the law to the facts as they are set out. You are deciding concrete cases, just as a jury does. Then, you get a chance to sit in judgment of the jury and examine the trial decision. You then decide whether the legal principles are fair or justified or indeed logical.

You don't need to be a lawyer to enjoy this section or to get the "right" answers. In fact, some lawyers may be at a disadvantage. The process of legal reasoning is no different from that of any other type of reasoning. Care, common sense and imagination should lead to the correct solution in most cases, regardless of previous education or training.

The law is fascinating, particularly when it is stripped down to the essential issues of right and wrong, common sense and nonsense. Our experience has shown that the cases contained in these pages will stimulate, provoke and amuse you. We hope that you have fun with them.

QUESTIONS OF LAW

The law states that "an assault is committed when a person unlawfully applies force to another person or creates in the mind of that other person a reasonable apprehension of the unlawful application of force."

The Lady and the Lecher

The unescorted young lady was walking down a road to go to work. The hopeful lecher drove by her very slowly and leered at her. He stopped his car, got out, and watched her until she was out of sight. The young lady was badly frightened by the experience.

Is the hopeful lecher guilty of assault?

Trial Court Decision: page 235
Appeal Court Decision: page 249

A Fig By Any Other Name

Paul gave Jane a fig to eat. Paul had amorous intentions towards Jane. In order to encourage her, Paul put a drug (thought to be an aphrodisiac) into the fig. Jane became very ill, discovered the tampering with the fig, and now lays a charge of assault against Paul.

Is Paul guilty of assault?

Trial Court Decision: page 239
Appeal Court Decision: page 253

Flash Fire

John negligently caused a flash fire in a restaurant. An employee activated an extinguisher, which caused a hissing sound. On hearing the sound, a customer shouted that gas was escaping and that there would be an explosion. The customers stampeded and Harry was injured in the stampede. Harry sued John for damages.

Does Harry succeed?

Trial Court Decision: page 243
Appeal Court Decision: page 251

Cutthroat Law

Shortal spent the night at the house of his friends, the Blakelys. Upon returning from errands, the Blakelys found Shortal in the kitchen. Shortal had cut his throat. The Blakelys were both violently shocked and upset, and they sue Shortal's estate for damages for shock and nervousness.

Will the Blakelys succeed?

Trial Court Decision: page 237
Appeal Court Decision: page 255

Many Are Called—Few Answer

Ron rented a canoe to Tim, who went out in it. The canoe overturned and Tim, now deceased, called for help. Ron heard the calls but ignored them. Tim's estate sues Ron.

Does Tim's estate recover?

Trial Court Decision: page 241
Appeal Court Decision: page 257

A law states that "a private communication that has been intercepted is inadmissible as evidence against the originator of the communication, unless the originator or the person intended by the originator to receive it has expressly consented to the admission thereof."

Oh, God!

Victor was charged with arson. He was brought into a room where he was left alone. While being watched and taped, he got down on his knees and said: "Oh, God, let me get away with it just this once."

Is this conversation admissible in evidence?

Trial Court Decision: page 246
Appeal Court Decision: page 260

The Sword or the Scalpel?

Louis stabbed the victim. The victim died of pneumonia because of negligent medical treatment of the stab wound. Louis was charged with murder.

Is Louis guilty of murder?

Trial Court Decision: page 235
Appeal Court Decision: page 258

Taking the Law
Into His Own Hands

Dean shot the victim (now deceased) in the abdomen. The wound was mortal and would have caused death within one hour, but before then the deceased slit his own throat. The throat wound would normally result in death after five minutes. Dean is charged with murder.

Is Dean guilty?

Trial Court Decision: page 239
Appeal Court Decision: page 262

Pen Pals

The charge is murder. The defense is insanity. The defense tries to place in evidence letters written by the accused, while in a psychiatric hospital, to Pope Pius XII, the FBI, the Secret Service and Walter Winchell.

Are these letters admissible in evidence?

Trial Court Decision: page 244
Appeal Court Decision: page 264

The Other Woman

Lucy sued for divorce. Her husband, Mac, also sued for divorce in the same lawsuit. Mac, however, refused to answer questions about his relationship with the "other woman." Mac's position is that he does not have to testify about his own wrongdoing because that would violate his privilege against self-incrimination.

Must Mac testify about the "other woman" if he wishes to pursue his suit for divorce?

Trial Court Decision: page 237
Appeal Court Decision: page 268

The Naked Truth?

The police placed Edmund in a police lineup. They also seized physical evidence from Edmund, took his fingerprints, took his photograph while he was in custody, and required that Edmund remove his clothing for identification purposes.

Did the police in any way violate Edmund's privilege against self-incrimination?

Trial Court Decision: page 241
Appeal Court Decision: page 266

Twice Cruel

Natalie sues for divorce. Can Natalie place in evidence the fact that her husband was divorced by a former wife for cruelty?

Trial Court Decision: page 246
Appeal Court Decision: page 270

The Belligerent Victim

The defense is self-defense. Dennis, the accused,

seeks to show that the deceased had a reputation for violence. Dennis argues that this evidence would show that the deceased, more likely than not, was the first aggressor.

Is the evidence admissible?

Trial Court Decision: page 235
Appeal Court Decision: page 272

The Case of
the Slippery Floor

Marsha fell on a terrazzo floor rendered slippery by rain. The defense seeks to show that no complaint about anyone slipping had been received during fifteen years though 4,000 to 5,000 people entered the store every day.

Can the defense show this?

Trial Court Decision: page 239
Appeal Court Decision: page 276

Shocking Pictures

In a criminal trial, pictures of the victim are tendered as evidence. The defense objects because the pictures are shocking and therefore might inflame the jury.

Are the pictures admissible?

Trial Court Decision: page 244
Appeal Court Decision: page 279

Stabbed and
Twice Dropped

Mildred stabbed the victim. The victim was transported to the hospital. The victim was twice dropped by the person carrying him. The hospital had no facilities for blood transfusions. Had the victim received blood, he would have had a 75 percent chance of survival. Mildred is charged with murder.

Is Mildred guilty?

Trial Court Decision: page 237
Appeal Court Decision: page 274

Buying Votes?

The jury was allowed outside the courtroom to view the scene of the accident. After the view, one of the people involved in the lawsuit entertained the jury in a local saloon. The other side in the case discovered this and asked for a mistrial.

Did the court order a mistrial?

Trial Court Decision: page 242
Appeal Court Decision: page 277

Serendipity in the Third

Police raided a bookie joint. During the raid, a phone call is taken by an officer. The caller says: "Put $100 on Serendipity in the third." At the trial, the prosecution tries to put this call in evidence. The defense objects and alleges that it is hearsay.

Is the evidence admissible?
Trial Court Decision: page 246
Appeal Court Decision: page 281

A Bad Reference

Employers are generally liable for the negligence of their employees. Otto, an employer, is sued by Jane for injuries Jane sustained as the result of Floyd's negligence. Floyd is an employee of Otto. Jane proposes to call witnesses to testify that Otto's foreman had complained before the accident of Floyd's incompetence. Otto claims that the complaints are hearsay.

Is the evidence admissible?
Trial Court Decision: page 235
Appeal Court Decision: page 249

The Unsuccessful Pickpocket

Connie put her hand in the victim's pocket. The victim grabbed Connie's wrist while her hand was in the pocket. The charge is attempted theft. There was no money in the pocket.

Is Connie guilty?
Trial Court Decision: page 239
Appeal Court Decision: page 253

Fear of Fleeing

The charge is murder. The prosecution wants to

show that, at a time after the murder, the accused, Polly, was arrested for reckless driving. Polly attempted to bribe the arresting officer and eventually she escaped. The defense argues that this evidence is not relevant to the murder charge.

Is the evidence admissible?

Trial Court Decision: page 244
Appeal Court Decision: page 251

The Employer's Wrath

A newspaper is sued for libel. The victim of the libel wants to prove that the newspaper fired the reporter who wrote the story shortly after it appeared. The lawyer for the newspaper claims that this should be inadmissible on the grounds that it is not relevant.

Is the evidence of the firing admissible?

Trial Court Decision: page 237
Appeal Court Decision: page 255

Her Husband Did It

In a murder trial, a witness called by the prosecution will testify that the victim (the wife of the physician-defendant) had said to a nurse, "My husband has poisoned me."

Is this statement admissible?

Trial Court Decision: page 242
Appeal Court Decision: page 257

Stop the Bus!

In a trial resulting from a collision between a bus and another vehicle, the victim calls a witness who was a passenger on the bus. The witness will say that the driver exclaimed, just before the collision, "I have no brakes" The defense lawyer claims that this statement is inadmissible as hearsay.

Is the statement admissible?

Trial Court Decision: page 246
Appeal Court Decision: page 261

Possession of a Firearm

Darlene was charged under two separate laws with possession of a firearm. The possible sentences under each law were different, but the facts necessary to support a conviction were the same.

Can Darlene be charged with and convicted of both offenses?

Trial Court Decision: page 235
Appeal Court Decision: page 259

Armed Robbery

Leander was charged with armed robbery and with using a firearm to commit an offense. Both charges arose out of the same robbery.

Can Leander be tried and convicted of both offenses?

Trial Court Decision: page 240
Appeal Court Decision: page 262

Speedy Trial

An accused is entitled to a speedy trial. Roxane was acquitted because the prosecution took too long to bring the case to trial.

Can Roxane be tried again for the same offense?

Trial Court Decision: page 244
Appeal Court Decision: page 264

Expensive Upgrade

Cedric leased a parcel of land to Montgomery. Montgomery was allowed to carry away sand and gravel, but he was required to leave the land at a uniform grade. Montgomery left the land at an uneven grade. It will cost $100,000 to grade the land properly. The land, however, is only worth $25,000 when properly graded.

Can Cedric recover the $100,000 from Montgomery to grade the land?

Trial Court Decision: page 237
Appeal Court Decision: page 268

A Misfire

Alan's barn caught fire. Alan called the police

inspector and asked for a fire truck. The inspector phoned the wrong fire station, one outside the jurisdiction in which Alan's barn was located. The station sent a truck. Everyone thought the fire station was inside the proper jurisdiction, but it wasn't. There is a fee for fighting fires outside the jurisdiction of the fire station, so the fire station sent Alan a bill for services rendered.

Does Alan have to pay despite the common error?

Trial Court Decision: page 242
Appeal Court Decision: page 266

The Right Charge

Eunice switched price tags on an article of clothing. She proceeded to the check-out counter and paid the price indicated on the switched tag. Eunice was later arrested and charged with theft. The defense argues that this was not a theft but rather a fraud, since Eunice had concluded a contract for the purchase of the article but under false pretenses.

Is Eunice guilty of theft?

Trial Court Decision: page 246
Appeal Court Decision: page 270

Hair Today and Tomorrow

A hair removal clinic offered to permanently remove facial hair. It advertises that the results are guaranteed. In response to the ads, Shirley went to the clinic and paid for the treatment. Shirley's hair loss was not permanent and she sued for breach of contract.

Did Shirley win?

Trial Court Decision: page 235
Appeal Court Decision: page 272

The Tired Lawyer

Rose was represented by a very tired lawyer. Indeed, the lawyer slept through a substantial portion of Rose's trial. Rose was found guilty. Rose appealed. Rose could not, however, point to any actual harm to her case because of her lawyer's naps.

Should Rose's appeal be allowed?

Trial Court Decision: page 240
Appeal Court Decision: page 276

Child neglect is defined as "leaving, with criminal negligence, a child unattended in or at any place for such period of time as may be likely to endanger the health or welfare of such child." The words "criminal negligence" mean that "a person fails to be aware of substantial and unjustifiable risk that the result will occur or that the circumstance exists."

Child Neglect?

Isabel had two children, aged eight and twenty-two months. She left the children alone to go to a party at a local tavern. While she was away, the children were killed in a fire, the cause of which is unknown. Isabel is charged with child neglect.

Is she guilty?

Trial Court Decision: page 244
Appeal Court Decision: page 280

Unwarranted Measures?

The police obtained a search warrant in the belief that Morton had heroin in his possession. Morton's door had an outer iron gate that could be left locked until Morton decided whether to let a caller in. The police were afraid that if they told Morton about the warrant, he might leave the gate locked and destroy the evidence. To avoid this, they forged an arrest warrant on fictitious traffic offenses and showed it to Morton. Morton let the police in to clear up the "mistake." Then they showed him the search warrant and found heroin. Morton is charged with possession of heroin. He argues that the search was illegal.

Is Morton found guilty?

Trial Court Decision: page 238
Appeal Court Decision: page 274

Leader of the Pact

Alex and Brett were unhappy youths. They made

a suicide pact. To carry out the pact, Alex drove his car over a cliff, with Brett as his passenger. Brett died. Alex recovered. Alex is charged with murder.

Is Alex guilty?

Trial Court Decision: page 242
Appeal Court Decision: page 278

A law concerning "ambulance-chasing" provides that it is an offense for a lawyer to solicit a person who has been injured in an accident, if the soliciting is for the purpose of commencing legal proceedings for that person.

Ambulance-Chasing

Fabian heard that Mr. Jones had been injured in an accident. He thought that Jones had a good negligence case, and talked to him about starting a lawsuit. Fabian is charged under the law and argues that the law is invalid because it is too broad and because it prohibits freedom of speech.

Is Fabian guilty?

Trial Court Decision: page 246
Appeal Court Decision: page 282

Caution—Inflammable!

Larry, an engineer, decided to apply a floor sealer in his recreation room. He did not extinguish the pilot light on his gas furnace in the adjacent room. It caused an explosion when the vapors from the sealer came in contact with it. Larry was seriously injured and sued the manufacturer of the sealer for negligence because the warning on the sealer stated only "Keep Away From Fire, Heat and Open-Flame Lights" and "Caution Inflammable! Keep Away From Open Flame!"

Is Larry's lawsuit successful?

Trial Court Decision: page 236
Appeal Court Decision: page 250

"This Is a Constable, Constable"

Curtis purchased a painting at a well-known art gallery. The painting was by the artist Constable. Five years later, Curtis discovered that the painting was not by Constable.

Can Curtis get his money back?

Trial Court Decision: page 240
Appeal Court Decision: page 254

Off-Duty?

A police officer was working, while off-duty, at a rock concert. He was in uniform and was working with the knowledge and consent of his superiors but was being paid by the concert promoters. Richmond assaulted the police officer and was charged with assaulting an officer. Richmond argues that he did not assault someone who was working as an officer but only a private security guard.

Is Richmond guilty?
> *Trial Court Decision: page 244*
> *Appeal Court Decision: page 254*

Sealed Bag

A government informer contacted John, informing him that cocaine was available for purchase. John said that he had $22,000 and that he would meet with the informer the next day. When John met with the informer, an undercover police officer was present. The officer took John to a nearby hotel room where John asked to see the cocaine. The officer left the room and returned with a sealed bag. The officer refused to open the bag, but John would only produce his money if the bag were opened. They argued for several minutes and John left. He was arrested shortly thereafter and charged with attempting to possess cocaine with the intent to distribute.

Is John guilty?
> *Trial Court Decision: page 238*
> *Appeal Court Decision: page 255*

Tavern License

Wally was a waiter in a tavern. He served alcohol to a minor, contrary to law. Wally entered into plea negotiations and agreed to plead guilty in return for the state agreeing "that it will not take further action by way of hearing before any court, or agency for action arising out of this transaction." After Wally's plea and conviction, Wally's employer, the owner of the tavern, was notified of a hearing before the local liquor licensing board to consider revocation of his tavern owner's license. The tavern owner argues that the state cannot revoke his license because of its agreement with Wally.

Can the tavern owner's license be revoked?

Trial Court Decision: page 242
Appeal Court Decision: page 257

Burgled Burglar?

Alfredo was charged with burglary. A witness who chased him testified that the thief was wearing a white tee shirt with an emblem on the back, blue jeans and tennis shoes, and that he ran across a patch of red gravel. When Alfredo was booked, the police placed his clothes in a personal property bag. At the trial, Alfredo asked that his clothing be produced, in order to show that he was not the thief. When the bag was opened, no shoes or pants were found. Alfredo asks that the charge be dismissed on the basis that important evidence has been lost by the prosecution.

Should the charge be dismissed?

Trial Court Decision: page 247
Appeal Court Decision: page 261

A law provides that certain communications between social workers and their clients are privileged and can therefore not be disclosed. The privilege applies to information given to the social worker "in his professional capacity that was necessary to enable him to render services in his professional capacity."

Dial M for Murder

Herbert is charged with murder. At 5:00 A.M., he phoned a psychiatric social worker with whom he had consulted on several prior occasions. Herbert told the social worker that he had just killed someone, and that he understood that the police would have to be notified. Herbert then gave his address.

Is the telephone conversation privileged within the meaning of the law?

Trial Court Decision: page 236
Appeal Court Decision: page 259

Discount Theft?

Timothy stole four men's suits. He is charged with theft over $200.00. The only evidence of the value of the suits was given by the security guard who arrested Timothy. The guard admitted that he got the price of the suits from the price tags, which indicated a price of $300.00.

Is Timothy guilty of theft over $200.00?

Trial Court Decision: page 240
Appeal Court Decision: page 263

Rapid Fire

Linda was shot three times. A witness heard the shots, went to help Linda and reached her within seconds of the shooting. The witness asked Linda who shot her and Linda replied that Carol had shot her. Carol is charged with murder.

Can the witness testify as to what Linda told him?

Trial Court Decision: page 244
Appeal Court Decision: page 265

A defendant is entitled to be presumed innocent until proven guilty.

Not Presumed Innocent

A prosecutor made the following comments in front of a jury: "You are to go through the trial with the presumption of innocence, and you should retain that attitude up through that point. But once you walk into that jury room you no longer have that responsibility—that mantle of the presumption of innocence; once you get into that jury room you no longer have to leave that mantle about his shoulders. You have the right to take it off."

Is the above statement sufficient to result in a mistrial?

Trial Court Decision: page 238
Appeal Court Decision: page 269

Double Dose of Cyanide

Henry was a goldsmith. He used potassium cyanide in his trade. Henry's wife died of potassium cyanide poisoning. Henry is charged with the murder of his wife. At his trial, the prosecution wants to show that Henry's previous wife had died, three years earlier, of potassium cyanide poisoning. Henry objects, claiming that this evidence would unfairly prejudice him in the eyes of the jury. There is no direct evidence that Henry administered the poison to either wife.

Is the evidence of the earlier poisoning admissible?

Trial Court Decision: page 242
Appeal Court Decision: page 267

Before a confession can be admitted as evidence, the prosecution must show that it has been given freely and voluntarily, without fear of threat or violence.

The Ends Justify the Means?

Jake kidnapped a young girl. He was arrested while trying to collect the ransom. Jake's accomplice was apparently holding the young girl at gunpoint and the police were most anxious to discover her location. The police choked Jake, twisted his arm behind his back and physically abused him until he revealed the girl's whereabouts. After Jake told the police where the girl was, he gave them a complete confession. The prosecution seeks to put the confession in evidence but the defense argues that Jake's confession was involuntary because of the violence used by the police.

Is Jake's confession admissible?

Trial Court Decision: page 247
Appeal Court Decision: page 271

Unfaded Memory

An elderly married couple was met in their dining room by a man holding a hatchet. The man struck them, robbed, bound and gagged them. That same evening, each member of the couple independently viewed six photographs. They each identified Mario as the robber. At the trial, however, neither the husband nor the wife could identify Mario in person. The prosecution relied on the fact that they had identified Mario by means of photographs.

Is this evidence sufficient to convict Mario of the offense?

Trial Court Decision: page 236
Appeal Court Decision: page 273

You Can Rely on Us

The accountants prepared financial statements for a client so that he could obtain financing from the bank. The accountants were negligent in the preparation of the statements. The bank had no relationship with the accountants, but the bank relied on the statements. The client went bankrupt. The bank sues the accountants.

Does the bank succeed?

Trial Court Decision: page 240
Appeal Court Decision: page 276

The law provides that a person is guilty of robbery in the first degree if that person "attempts to kill anyone or purposely inflicts or attempts to inflict serious bodily harm, or is armed with or uses or threatens the immediate use of a deadly weapon."

Less Than Meets the Eye

Jim robbed a woman in a parking lot. He had his hand in his coat pocket and pretended that he was concealing a revolver. The woman believed that Jim had a revolver, but Jim in fact had none. Jim is charged with robbery in the first degree.

Is he guilty of robbery in the first degree?

Trial Court Decision: page 245
Appeal Court Decision: page 280

Convenience Store Mugging

Alice went shopping at a convenience store operated by the Acme Corporation. Alice was mugged in the well-lighted parking lot and sustained injuries. In the year preceding Alice's mugging, seven other muggings had occurred in the parking lot of the same store. Acme hired a security guard, but he was inside the store when Alice was assaulted. Alice sues Acme for failure to warn and for failure to provide adequate security.

Is Alice successful?

Trial Court Decision: page 238
Appeal Court Decision: page 275

Policing the Police

Alphonse, a police officer, was required by the Police Department to carry his gun at all times within city limits. He returned home one day, shot his wife and committed suicide. The wife suffered brain damage and now sues the Police Department for negligence. The wife argues that the Police Department failed to adopt an effective program of psychological screening of police officers. The Department had tried several psychological programs in an effort to screen out emotionally unstable officers, but these had proven ineffective and had been abandoned.

Is the Police Department guilty of negligence?

Trial Court Decision: page 242
Appeal Court Decision: page 278

Unfinished Business

Boris and Charlie were caught behind a liquor store during the early morning hours. Boris and Charlie had broken approximately halfway through the store's rear wall. They are charged with breaking and entering with intent to steal.

Are they guilty?
Trial Court Decision: page 247
Appeal Court Decision: page 282

Kidnapping Jenny's Daughter

Michael conspired with an accomplice, Jenny, to take her daughter from a child welfare agency. Jenny took the child from the agency at gunpoint. Michael is charged with conspiring to kidnap the child. The law provides that a parent cannot be convicted of kidnapping her child. Michael is not a parent.

Is Michael guilty?
Trial Court Decision: page 236
Appeal Court Decision: page 250

The Wrong Parts

Harold was employed by an airline and had the authority to order parts. He bought and caused to be delivered car parts that could not be used by the airline but could be used on his own car. Other employees of the airline owned the same make of car as Harold. Harold is charged with embezzling automobile parts.

Is Harold guilty?
Trial Court Decision: page 240
Appeal Court Decision: page 254

A Gift of Hacksaw Blades

Gerrard was a prison inmate. His devoted girl-friend, Dawn, visited him. She was anxious to see him free and, in order to help him escape, passed him four hacksaw blades. An attentive guard saw Dawn pass Gerrard the blades, and after a search, seized them. Gerrard is charged with attempted escape.

Is Gerrard guilty?

Trial Court Decision: page 245
Appeal Court Decision: page 252

The Defense of Diligence

Peter abandoned his wife and children. The wife worked two jobs and was aided by her family and local church. Both the wife and children had adequate food and shelter. Peter made no payments to the wife. He is charged with criminal nonsupport of his children. In order for the prosecution to gain a conviction, it must show that the children were in "necessitous circumstances" at the relevant time.

Is Peter guilty?

Trial Court Decision: page 238
Appeal Court Decision: page 256

Too Late for Pistol-Packing

Sally wanted to bring her revolver with her to New York. She had a New York license to carry the pistol. Sally arrived at the Chicago airport but she was too late to check the suitcase that contained her revolver. She was told to go to the gate with her luggage. As Sally went through the x-ray machine, the alarm went off and the gun was discovered.

Is Sally guilty of attempting to board an aircraft while having a gun in her possession?

Trial Court Decision: page 243
Appeal Court Decision: page 256

The Joke's on You!

Morris had been drinking when he entered the bank. "I have a .38 in my pocket," he said to the teller, "and I want all your money." The teller set off a silent alarm. But when she handed Morris the cash, he said he had been joking all along. He left the bank empty-handed and was arrested.

Is Morris guilty of attempted robbery?

Trial Court Decision: page 247
Appeal Court Decision: page 261

Choose Your Weapon Carefully

Alexander robbed a store while armed with a B-B gun. The B-B gun looked like a .45 caliber semi-automatic pistol but fired B-Bs by means of a spring. Alexander is charged with using a firearm in the commission of a criminal offense. The word "firearm" is not defined in the law. Alexander argues that "firearm" should be defined as a weapon that fires a projectile by means of gunpowder.

Is Alexander guilty?

Trial Court Decision: page 236
Appeal Court Decision: page 260

Intoxication Plus

Ralph killed a bicycle rider while driving his truck. There was no evidence that Ralph's driving was noticeably bad. Ralph's blood test however indicated that he had a blood-alcohol level of .16%. The law provided that a .10% blood-alcohol level was evidence of intoxication, absent proof to the contrary.

Can Ralph be convicted of causing death by criminal negligence?

Trial Court Decision: page 240
Appeal Court Decision: page 263

Practical Joker

Morris was the mischievous sort. As a practical joke, he bent a stop sign at an intersection. Bill was driving through the intersection, could not see the stop sign, and collided with Colleen's car. Colleen was killed in the crash. Morris is charged with negligent homicide.

Is Morris guilty?

Trial Court Decision: page 245
Appeal Court Decision: page 265

Take the Money and Run

An insurance company paid a widow money
under an insurance policy on her husband's life.
They did so by mistake, since the policy had lapsed
for non-payment of premiums.

Can the widow keep the money?

Trial Court Decision: page 238
Appeal Court Decision: page 269

The Fatal Hostage

Steve and Tim took Caroline hostage while
attempting to escape from an armed robbery. The
police arrived and during a pitched battle with Steve
and Tim, Caroline was shot and killed by the police.
Steve and Tim are charged with the "felony murder"
of Caroline. They argue that they cannot be held
responsible for the death of Caroline since the police
caused the death of Caroline, not Steve or Tim.

Are they guilty of murder?

Trial Court Decision: page 243
Appeal Court Decision: page 267

She Never Heard of Henry

Henry never paid his traffic tickets. There were
several warrants outstanding against him. One day,
Henry's car was parked in front of Kate's house.
Police knocked at Kate's door and asked for Henry.
Kate said that she had never heard of him. Unde-

terred, the police looked through a window and saw Henry hiding in the basement. They arrested him. Kate is charged with hampering or impeding a public official in the performance of his lawful duties?

Is Kate guilty?

Trial Court Decision: page 247
Appeal Court Decision: page 271

Under the law relating to "criminal simulation" an offense is committed if an object is made or altered so as to have an appearance of "antiquity, rarity, source, or authorship" that it does not in fact have.

Mass Produced

Avery sold Bryce a one-jewel watch that had a famous trademark on it. Avery told Bryce that the watch was a genuine seventeen-jewel watch when in fact it was not. Avery is charged with "criminal simulation"

Is he guilty of the offense?

Trial Court Decision: page 236
Appeal Court Decision: page 273

Cruise Control

Pierre had to drive long distances because of his work. He liked to use the automatic cruise control. He set the control at the speed limit but was nevertheless ticketed for speeding. At his trial, he showed that the automatic cruise control had malfunctioned on the day in question.

Is Pierre guilty of speeding?

Trial Court Decision: page 240
Appeal Court Decision: page 276

Once or Forever?

Daniel was a police officer. One day he decided to keep a coat that he knew had been stolen. Thirteen months later he was charged with improper conduct in office. There is no doubt that receipt of the stolen coat was improper conduct in office. But a prosecution for such an offense must begin less than twelve months after the alleged crime. The prosecution argues that possession of the coat by Daniel was a continuing offense committed every day during the thirteen months, and that therefore the twelve month statute of limitations had not expired. But the defense argues that the prosecution was begun too late.

Is Daniel guilty?

Trial Court Decision: page 243
Appeal Court Decision: page 280

Murder, She Said

Abigail and Barney were cut-throat competitors. Unable to eliminate a business rival by legitimate means, they decided to have him killed. Abigail flew to New York and met with an undercover police officer. Abigail offered the officer $2,500.00 to murder the rival. The officer agreed and Abigail said that she would mail him the rival's photograph, a map of his cottage and the fee. Several days later, Abigail called off the murder.

Is Abigail guilty of conspiracy to commit murder?
Trial Court Decision: page 238
Appeal Court Decision: page 275

Illegal Search?

Earl grew marijuana on his farm. Narcotics agents drove to Earl's farm, passed his house, and came upon a locked gate with a "no trespassing" sign. The agents used a footpath to walk around the gate and found a field of marijuana about one mile from Earl's house. The agents had no warrant. Earl is charged with cultivating marijuana and argues that the search is illegal.

Is the evidence admissible?
Trial Court Decision: page 243
Appeal Court Decision: page 278

On-the-Job Training

Lloyd was charged with a complicated mail fraud. His lawyer withdrew just before the trial and the court appointed a young lawyer with a real estate practice to defend Lloyd. The lawyer had never handled a jury trial and was allowed only twenty-five days to prepare, although the prosecution had taken four and a half years to investigate the case. Lloyd is convicted and appeals on the basis that his lawyer was young, inexperienced and had been given too little time to prepare, given the complexity of the case.

Is Lloyd's appeal successful?

Trial Court Decision: page 247
Appeal Court Decision: page 282

The Lawyer Was Wrong

Oliver was charged with a criminal offense. The penalty for the offense was fixed by law to a period of ten years. Oliver's lawyer told him that he would be entitled to parole after three years. On the basis of this advice, Oliver pleaded guilty. Unfortunately, his lawyer had been wrong about the parole. Oliver was only eligible for parole after seven years. Oliver was understandably quite perturbed and he now seeks to change his plea and be awarded a new trial.

Is Oliver entitled to a new trial?

Trial Court Decision: page 236
Appeal Court Decision: page 250

The Accompanist

Munroe was the manager of a popular singer. Munroe thought that Glen, a pianist, had agreed to accompany the singer at a forthcoming concert. Munroe issued posters and programs that showed Glen as pianist for the singer's performance. In fact,

Glen had not agreed to accompany the singer. As a result of the posters, Glen lost another contract, because people believed that Glen was unavailable.

Can Glen recover damages because of the statements in the poster?

Trial Court Decision: page 241
Appeal Court Decision: page 254

Inlaw Outlaw

Debby was a two-year old infant. Philamena was Debby's aunt-in-law (the widow of a brother of Debby's mother). Philamena obtained insurance on Debby's life from an insurance company. Philamena named herself beneficiary. The insurance company should not have issued the policy to Philamena, because Philamena had no "insurable interest" in the life of Debby (Debby and Philamena were not closely enough related). Philamena murdered Debby in order to collect on the insurance policy. Debby's father sues the insurance company for negligently issuing the policy to Philamena.

Should Debby's father be successful?

Trial Court Decision: page 245
Appeal Court Decision: page 252

Water Works

During construction work, Albert negligently broke a street water main causing a loss in water pressure. The city was very slow in repairing the main and, after a time when repairs ought to have been made by the city, Pierre's house caught on fire. Pierre's house burned down because of the low water pressure.

Can Pierre successfully sue Albert?

Trial Court Decision: page 239
Appeal Court Decision: page 256

A criminal statute defines the offense of perjury as follows: "Every one commits perjury who, being a witness in a judicial proceeding, with intent to mislead gives false evidence, knowing that the evidence is false."

No Harm, No Foul?

Marcel lied on the stand with intent to mislead. The trial court disregarded Marcel's evidence which did not figure in its verdict. Marcel is charged with perjury.

Is Marcel guilty?

Trial Court Decision: page 243
Appeal Court Decision: page 258

The Distracted Mother

Mary was a distracted mother. She did not carefully supervise her four-year-old son, Kerr. Kerr ran out from between parked cars and was struck by Gustave. The court appointed a guardian for Kerr. The guardian sues both Mary and Gustave for negligence.

Is Mary responsible in damage for negligently supervising Kerr?

Trial Court Decision: page 248
Appeal Court Decision: page 262

Horse Sense

Nicole accused Reginald of acts of cruelty to a horse, including beating the horse and knocking out an eye. Reginald accused Nicole of slander. At the trial, Nicole showed that Reginald had in fact been cruel to the horse, but could not show that the horse's eye had been knocked out.

Is Reginald entitled to damages for slander?

Trial Court Decision: page 237
Appeal Court Decision: page 260

Fool's Gold

Duncan was a kind soul, but not very clever. A fortune teller told him that a pot of gold could be found on his land. Ned, a practical joker, buried a pot on Duncan's land which he "discovered" in Duncan's presence. Duncan took the pot to the local bank and opened it, in front of a howling, jeering crowd. Duncan suffered deep mental suffering and humiliation.

Can Duncan recover damages from Ned?
Trial Court Decision: page 241
Appeal Court Decision: page 264

The constitution of the United States provides freedom of speech and freedom of the press. But the law also provides the right to be free from defamatory attacks against a person's reputation. What happens when these freedoms come into conflict?

Sign of the Times

Steve was an elected commissioner of the city of Montgomery, Alabama. Steve was responsible for supervising the police department. Lowell was a black clergyman who paid for an ad in the New York Times that accused Steve of persecuting civil rights activists in Alabama. The ad contained several inaccuracies of fact and Steve sued for defamation. The Times had printed the ad, without checking its accuracy, on the strength of Lowell's reputation.

Was Steve successful?
Trial Court Decision: page 245
Appeal Court Decision: page 265

Bad Publicity

Millie was a wealthy socialite married to Johnny. Millie sued Johnny for divorce. The divorce trial was messy and very public. Evidence was one of extra-marital activity on both sides, but the judge discounted much of it. *Hour* magazine carelessly got its facts wrong. In its "Milestones" column, it wrote the divorce had been granted on "grounds of extreme cruelty and adultery... The seventeen-month intermittent trial produced enough testimony of extramarital adventures on both sides, said the judge, to make Dr. Freud's hair curl." Millie sues *Hour* magazine, which alleges that Millie was a public figure and that it is not liable for defamation in the absence of evidence of actual malice.

Should Millie be successful in her action for defamation?

Trial Court Decision: page 239
Appeal Court Decision: page 269

The law provides that: "One who gives publicity to matters concerning the private life of another, of a kind highly offensive to a reasonable man, is subject to liability to the other for invasion of his privacy."

Invasion of Privacy?

Val was something of a spendthrift. His credit card was always over the limit. The credit card company became fed up and sent Val's account to the collection agency. The collection agency was aggressive. It telephoned Val's relatives. It wrote to Val's employer. The collection agency was not offensive, but it did discuss Val's debt with the person that it contacted.

Can Val recover damages for invasion of privacy?

Trial Court Decision: page 243
Appeal Court Decision: page 267

In an insurance policy insuring against death by "external, violent and accidental means," the means of death must generally be accidental and independent of all other causes. While it is not always easy to determine whether a person has died by external, violent and accidental means, this determination is crucial to recovery under many life insurance policies.

The Fatal Trip

Abe was a chronic alcoholic. On his first day in the hospital, he had a convulsion while en route to the bathroom. He struck his head and died. Abe's trip to the bathroom was unsupervised by hospital staff.

Did Abe die by external, violent and accidental means?

Trial Court Decision: page 248
Appeal Court Decision: page 271

Blood Rights

Delores, 22 and unmarried, was severely injured

in a car accident. She was taken unconscious to a nearby hospital, badly needing a blood transfusion. Delores and her parents were Jehovah's Witnesses. The parents refused to consent to the transfusion. The hospital authorities go before a judge in order to obtain permission to give Delores a transfusion.

Can the judge authorize the transfusion?

Trial Court Decision: page 237
Appeal Court Decision: page 273

Tennis, Anyone?

Renee was a tennis player. She had played professional tennis as a male but, following a sex-change operation, she began to play as a female. Renee was very successful as a female tennis player. She wanted to play as a woman in the U.S. Open tournament. The tournament organizers decided to institute a chromosome test as a requirement for play. Renee could not, of course, pass this test even though she had all the sexual characteristics of a woman with the exception of the ability to bear children. Renee claims that the chromosome test violates her civil rights and that she should be considered a female. Renee seeks an injunction against the tournament organizers.

Should Renee be allowed to play?

Trial Court Decision: page 241
Appeal Court Decision: page 276

A Matter of Faith

Igor applied to the university. Before acceptance, the university required a vaccination. Igor refused. The university supplied Igor with a printed form that allowed an exemption from vaccination on religious grounds. The form required a statement that the person seeking the exemption was a member of the Christian Science faith. Igor was not a Christian Scientist, but nevertheless objected to the vaccination on religious grounds. The university turned down Igor's application because he refused vaccination. Igor sued.

Should Igor be admitted to the university?

Trial Court Decision: page 245
Appeal Court Decision: page 281

Home Cooking

Cynthia is charged with the murder of her husband by arsenic poisoning. There is no direct evidence against Cynthia. Cynthia, the husband, and their three sons lived together in the same house. Cynthia prepared their food and made tea for them. The prosecution seeks to prove that, after the husband's death, two sons died by arsenic poisoning and that the third became severely ill.

Can the prosecution place in evidence the death of the two sons?

Trial Court Decision: page 239
Appeal Court Decision: page 275

Cost Cutting

In response to the explosion of medical malpractice claims, a law was passed limiting recovery in court cases for malpractice to $500,000. Cora, a four-year-old child, was badly injured by a doctor's negligence. Cora's guardian sues for $2,000,000 and argues that the law limiting damages is invalid.

Is the law valid?

Trial Court Decision: page 243
Appeal Court Decision: page 279

The Good News
and the Bad News

Utility Insurance Company employed Dr. Smith to examine Irving, an applicant for insurance. Irving badly needed insurance, but was very sick. Irving conspired with Dr. Smith to submit a false medical report. Utility granted insurance to Irving on the basis of the false report. Irving died soon after and Utility paid his beneficiaries. Some time later, Utility discovered the fraud and sued Dr. Smith and Dr. Smith's medical malpractice insurer. The insurer was responsible for the doctor's "malpractice" and his "errors or mistakes."

Can Utility recover from Dr. Smith's insurer?

Trial Court Decision: page 248
Appeal Court Decision: page 283

TRIAL
COURT DECISIONS

The Lady and the Lecher
The hopeful lecher is guilty of assault.

The Sword or the Scalpel?
Louis is guilty of murder.

The Belligerent Victim
The evidence is admissible.

A Bad Reference
The evidence is admissible.

Possession of a Firearm
Darlene can be charged with and convicted of both offenses.

Hair Today and Tomorrow
Shirley did not win.

Caution—Inflammable!
Larry's suit is successful.

Dial M for Murder
The telephone conversation is not privileged within the meaning of the law

Unfaded Memory
This evidence is sufficient to convict Mario of the offense.

Kidnapping Jenny's Daughter
Michael is not guilty.

Choose Your Weapon Carefully
Alexander is not guilty

Mass Produced
Avery is not guilty of the offense.

The Lawyer Was Wrong
Oliver is entitled to a new trial.

Horse Sense
Reginald is not entitled to damages for slander.

Blood Rights
The Judge can authorize the transfusion.

Cutthroat Law
The Blakelys did not succeed.

The Other Woman
Mac need not testify about the "other woman."

Stabbed and Twice Dropped
Mildred is guilty.

The Employer's Wrath
The evidence is admissible.

Expensive Upgrade
Cedric can recover only $25,000 from Montgomery.

Unwarranted Measures?
Morton is found guilty

Sealed Bag
John is guilty.

Not Presumed Innocent
The statement is not sufficient to result in
a mistrial.

Convenience Store Mugging
Alice is successful.

The Defense of Diligence
Peter is not guilty.

Take the Money and Run
The widow cannot keep the money.

Murder, She Said
Abigail is guilty of conspiring to commit murder.

Water Works
Pierre can successfully sue Albert.

Bad Publicity
Millie should be successful in her action for defamation.

Home Cooking
The prosecution cannot place in evidence the death of the two sons.

A Fig By Any Other Name
Paul is guilty of assault.

Taking the Law Into His Own Hands
Dean is guilty.

The Case of the Slippery Floor
The defense cannot show this.

The Unsuccessful Pickpocket
Connie is guilty.

Armed Robbery
Leander can be tried and convicted of both offenses.

The Tired Lawyer
Rose's appeal should be allowed.

"This Is a Constable, Constable"
Curtis cannot get his money back.

Discount Theft?
Timothy is guilty of theft over $200.

You Can Rely on Us
The bank does not succeed.

The Wrong Parts
Harold is not guilty

Intoxication Plus
Ralph cannot be convicted of causing death by criminal negligence.

Cruise Control
Pierre is guilty of speeding.

The Accompanist
Glen can recover damages because of the statements in the posters.

Fool's Gold
Duncan can recover damages from Ned.

Tennis, Anyone?
Renee should be allowed to play.

Many Are Called—Few Answer
Tim's estate does not recover.

The Naked Truth?
The police in no way violated Edmund's privilege against self-incrimination.

Buying Votes?
The court did not order a mistrial.

Her Husband Did It
The statement is admissible.

A Misfire
Alan has to pay despite the common error.

Leader of the Pact
Alex is not guilty.

Tavern License
The tavern owner's license can be revoked.

Double Dose of Cyanide
The evidence of the earlier poisoning is
admissible.

Policing the Police
The Police Department is guilty of negligence.

Too Late for Pistol-Packing
Sally is guilty of attempting to board an aircraft while having a gun in her possession.

The Fatal Hostage
They are guilty of murder.

Illegal Search?
The evidence is admissible.

No Harm, No Foul?
Marcel is not guilty of perjury.

Invasion of Privacy?
Val can recover damages for invasion of privacy.

Cost Cutting
The law is valid.

Flash Fire
Harry succeeds.

Pen Pals
These letters are not admissible in evidence.

Shocking Pictures
The pictures are admissible.

Fear of Fleeing
The evidence is admissible.

Speedy Trial
Roxane cannot be tried again for the same offense.

Child Neglect?
Isabel is guilty of child neglect.

Off-Duty?
Richmond is guilty.

Rapid Fire
The witness can testify as to what Linda told him.

Less Than Meets the Eye
Jim is guilty of robbery in the first degree.

A Gift of Hacksaw Blades
Gerrard is guilty

Practical Joker
Morris is not guilty.

Once or Forever?
Daniel is guilty

Inlaw Outlaw
Debby's father should be successful.

Sign of the Times
Steve was successful.

A Matter of Faith
Igor should be admitted to the university

Oh, God!
This conversation is not admissible in evidence.

Twice Cruel
Natalie can place in evidence the fact that her husband was divorced by a former wife for cruelty.

Serendipity in the Third
The evidence is admissible.

Stop the Bus!
The statement is admissible.

The Right Charge
Eunice is guilty of theft.

Ambulance-Chasing
Fabian is not guilty.

Burgled Burglar?
The charge should not be dismissed.

The Ends Justify the Means?
Jake's confession is admissible.

Unfinished Business
They are guilty.

The Joke's On You!
Morris is guilty of attempted robbery.

She Never Heard of Henry
Kate is guilty.

On-the-Job Training
Lloyd's appeal is successful.

The Distracted Mother
Mary is responsible in damages for negligent supervision.

The Fatal Trip
Abe died by external, violent and accidental means.

The Good News and the Bad News
Utility cannot recover from Dr. Smith's insurer.

APPEAL
COURT DECISIONS

The Lady and the Lecher

The hopeful lecher is not guilty of assault, because there was no overt act, no threat, no offer or attempt to injure. He cannot be convicted solely for what may have been in his mind.

State of North Carolina versus Ingram, decided by the Supreme Court of North Carolina, in February, 1953, decision rendered by Judge Armstrong.

Formal legal citation: 74 S.E. (2d) 532

A Bad Reference

The evidence is admissible, because the complaints were evidence of knowledge by Otto and his foreman of some defect in Floyd's work.

Borderland Coal Co. versus Kerns, decided by the Court of Appeals of Kentucky, in June, 1915, decision rendered by Judge Hurt.

Formal legal citation: 177 S. W. 266

Caution—Inflammable!

Larry's lawsuit is successful, because the warning on the sealer was not explicit enough.

Lambert versus Lastoplex Chemicals Co. Ltd., decided by a panel of five Judges of the Supreme Court of Canada, in December, 1971, decision rendered by Judge Laskin.

Formal legal citation: 25 D.L.R. (3d) 121 (Canada)

Kidnapping Jenny's Daughter

Michael is not guilty. To allow prosecution for conspiring to kidnap would frustrate the law's intent, which is to immunize parents from prosecution for kidnapping their own children.

Lythgoe versus the State of Alaska, decided by the Supreme Court of Alaska, in November, 1980, decision rendered by Judge Boochever.

Formal legal citation: 626 P. (2d) 1082

The Lawyer Was Wrong

Oliver is entitled to a new trial, because his plea was based on the erroneous advice of his lawyer. Oliver should be allowed to change his plea.

*O'Tuel versus Osborne, Attorney General of
North Carolina, decided by a panel of three
Judges of the United States Court of Appeals,
Fourth Circuit, in February, 1983, decision ren-
dered by Judge Sprouse.*
Formal legal citation: 706 F. (2d) 498

Flash Fire

Harry does not succeed, because the damages
were not reasonably foreseeable and were accord-
ingly too remote to justify recovery.

*Bradford versus Kanellos, decided by a panel of
three Judges of the Ontario Court of Appeal, in
December, 1970, decision rendered by Judge
Schroeder.*
*Formal legal citation: [1971] 2 OR. 393
(Canada)*

Fear of Fleeing?

The evidence is admissible. Evidence of flight is
generally admissible as evidence of guilt, though
not necessarily guilt of the crime charged.

*State of New Mexico versus Nelson, decided by
a panel of five Judges of the Supreme Court of
New Mexico, in March, 1959, decision rendered
by Judge Compton.*
Formal legal citation: 65 N.M. 403

Off-Duty?

Richmond is guilty, because the city and the public were obtaining real benefit from the officer's activities. Whether or not the officer was on duty does not matter.

State of New Jersey versus De Santo, decided by a panel of three Judges of the Superior Court of New Jersey, Appellate Division, in December, 1979, decision rendered by Judge Milmed.

Formal legal citation: 410 A. (2d) 704

A Gift of Hacksaw Blades

Gerrard is not guilty, since he did not act to put his escape plan into execution. Receipt of the blades was mere preparation.

Smith versus the State of Georgia, decided by a panel of three Judges of the Court of Appeals of Georgia, in October, 1980, decision rendered by Chief Judge Deen.

Formal legal citation: 275 S.E. (2d) 689

Inlaw Outlaw

Debby's father should be successful, because the insurance company created a situation of a kind that would have afforded temptation "to a recognizable percentage of humanity to commit murder."

Liberty National Life Insurance Co. versus Weldon, decided by a panel of five Judges of the Supreme Court of Alabama, in November, 1957, decision rendered by Judge Lawson, with Judge Coleman dissenting.

Formal legal citation: 100 So. (2d) 696

A Fig By Any Other Name

Paul is guilty of assault because he caused the injury. Force need not be applied directly in order to constitute assault.

Commonwealth (State of Massachusetts) versus Stratton, decided by a panel of the Court of Appeal, in November, 1873, decision rendered by Judge Wells.

Formal legal citation: 19 Am. Rep. 350

The Unsuccessful Pickpocket

Connie is guilty. The fact that the theft was impossible is not a defense to a charge of attempt.

R. versus Scott, decided by a panel of three Judges of the Alberta Supreme Court, Appellate Division, in November, 1963, decision rendered by Judge MacDonald.

Formal legal citation: [1964] 2 C.C.C. 257 (Canada)

"This Is A Constable, Constable"

Curtis cannot get his money back, because contracts cannot be kept open indefinitely; too much time had expired.

Leaf versus International Galleries, decided by a panel of three Judges of the King's Bench Division, in February, 1950, decision rendered by Judge Denning.

Formal legal citation: [1950] 2 KB. 86 (U.K.)

The Wrong Parts

Harold is not guilty, because the prosecution offered no evidence as to what happened to the parts after delivery. That the airline had no use for the parts is insufficient to support a conviction.

State of New Jersey versus Barbossa, decided by a panel of three Judges of the Superior Court of New Jersey, Appellate Division, in December, 1976, decision rendered by the panel, with Judge Seidman dissenting.

Formal legal citation: 384 A. (2d) 523

The Accompanist

Glen cannot recover damages because the statements in the posters contained no defamation (that is, no loss of reputation); neither were the words published maliciously.

Shapiro versus La Morta, decided by King's Bench Division, in October, 1923, decision rendered by Judge Lush.

Formal legal citation: 40 T.L.R. 39 (U.K.)

Cutthroat Law

The Blakelys did succeed, because Shortal should have anticipated the effect of his act upon the Blakelys.

Blakely versus Shortal, decided by a panel of Judges of the Supreme Court of Iowa, in October, 1945, decision rendered by Justice Mantz.

Formal legal citation: 20 N.W. (2d) 28

The Employer's Wrath

The evidence is not admissible. Evidence of measures taken after an incident is not generally admissible.

Turner versus Hearst, decided by a panel of three Judges of the Supreme Court of California, in December, 1896, decision rendered by Judge Henshaw.

Formal legal citation: 47 P. 129

Sealed Bag

John is not guilty, because he had made no substantial step towards the commission of the completed offense.

United States versus Joyce, decided by the United States Court of Appeals for the Eighth Circuit, in December, 1982.
Formal legal citation: 32 Cr. L. 2262

The Defense of Diligence

Peter is guilty, because the phrase "necessitous circumstances" should be interpreted to accomplish the legislature's intention of compelling spouses to support their children.

State of Kansas versus Knetzer, decided by a panel of three Judges of the Court of Appeals of Kansas, in September, 1979, decision rendered by Judge Abbott.
Formal legal citation: 600 P. (2d) 160

Water Works

Pierre can successfully sue Albert, because Albert's negligence was the cause of the low water pressure. Albert's liability is not affected by the city's failure to act.

Gilbert versus New Mexico Construction, decided by a panel of five Judges of the Supreme Court of New Mexico, in February, 1935, decision rendered by Judge Watson, with Judges Hudspeth and Beckley dissenting.
Formal legal citation: 44 P. (2d) 489

Many Are Called—Few Answer

Tim's estate does not recover, because there is no duty to rescue at common law.

Osterlind versus Hill, decided by a panel of Judges of the Supreme Judicial Court of Massachusetts, in March, 1928, decision rendered by Judge Braley.

Formal legal citation: 160 N.E. 301

Her Husband Did It

The statement is not admissible; it is classic hearsay.

Shepard versus United States of America, decided by the Supreme Court of the United States, in October, 1933, decision rendered by Judge Cardozo.

Formal legal citation: 290 U.S. 96

Tavern License

The tavern owner's license can be revoked, because the tavern owner was not a party to the plea negotiations or the subsequent agreement.

Northeast Motor Company, Inc. versus North Carolina State Board of Alcohol Control, decided by a panel of three Judges of the Court of Appeals of North Carolina, in March, 1978, decision rendered by Judge Martin.

Formal legal citation: 241 S.E. (2d) 727

Too Late for Pistol-Packing

Sally is guilty of attempting to board an aircraft while having a gun in her possession, because passing through a screening device must be considered an attempt to board the aircraft. The license to carry the gun had no bearing on a charge of attempting to board an aircraft.

The People of the State of Illinois versus Hysner, decided by a panel of three Judges of the Appellate Court of Illinois, First District, Fifth Division, in March, 1978, decision rendered by Justice Mejda.

Formal legal citation: 374 N.E. (2d) 799

No Harm, No Foul?

Marcel is guilty of perjury, because whether or not the court is actually misled is irrelevant. Only the intent to mislead is important.

Regina versus Regnier, decided by a panel of three Judges of the Ontario Court of Appeal, in February, 1955, decision rendered by Chief Justice of Ontario Pickup.

Formal legal citation: 21 C.R. 374 (Canada)

The Sword or the Scalpel?

Louis is not guilty of murder, because the death was not caused by the stab wound.

R. versus Jordan, decided by a panel of three Judges of the Court of Criminal Appeal, in August, 1956, decision rendered by Judge Hallett.

Formal legal citation. 40 Cr. App. R. 152 (England)

Possession of a Firearm

Darlene cannot be charged and convicted of both offenses. They were essentially identical, and it would be unfair if one set of facts could lead to conviction on both charges.

United States versus Girst, decided by the United States Court of Appeals, District of Columbia Circuit, in December, 1979, decision rendered by Judge MacKinnon.

Formal legal citation: F. (2d) 1014

Dial M for Murder

The telephone conversation is not privileged within the meaning of the law, because the conversation here showed that no confidentiality was intended, particularly since Herbert knew that the police would be called.

State of South Dakota versus Martin, decided by a panel of two Judges of the Supreme Court of South Dakota, in November, 1978, decision rendered by Judge Miller.

Formal legal citation: 274 N.W. (2d) 893

Choose Your Weapon Carefully

Alexander is guilty, since one of the purposes of the law is to protect victims from the fear of physical harm. The word firearm should be given its widest possible meaning.

Holloman versus The Commonwealth of Virginia, decided by a panel of seven Judges of the Supreme Court of Virginia, in August, 1980.

Formal legal citation: 269 S.E. (2d) 356

Horse Sense

Reginald is entitled to damages for slander, because the charge of knocking out an eye was an implication of a much greater cruelty than simply beating the horse. Since Nicole could not prove this act of cruelty, she was liable.

Weaver versus Lloyd, decided by the Court of King's Bench, in May, 1824.

Formal legal citation: 107 ER 535 (England)

Oh, God!

The conversation is admissible in evidence, because the court decided that, for the purpose of this law, God should not be considered to be a person.

*R. versus Davie, decided by the British Colum-
bia County Court, in May, 1979, decision rendered by Judge Lander.*
   Formal legal citation: 9 C.R. (3d) 275 (Canada)

Stop the Bus!
   The statement is admissible, because statements
made in the heat of the moment are generally
admissible.
   *Schwam versus Reece et al., decided by the
Supreme Court of Arkansas, in May, 1948, deci-
sion rendered by Justice Millwee.*
   Formal legal citation: 210 S.W. 903

Burgled Burglar?
   The charge should be dismissed, because the
evidence was lost to the prejudice of Alfredo.
   *Howard versus the State of Nevada, decided by
a panel of five Judges of the Supreme Court of
Nevada, in September, 1979, decision rendered by
Judge Young.*
   Formal legal citation: 600 P. (2d) 214

The Joke's on You!
   Morris is not guilty of attempted robbery, because
the evidence was equally consistent with no criminal intent as with intent that was abandoned.

Regina versus Mathe, decided by the British Columbia Court of Appeal, in April, 1973, decision rendered by Judge Maclean.
Formal legal citation: [1973] 4W.W.R. 483 (Canada)

The Distracted Mother
Mary is not legally responsible for negligently supervising Kerr, because a parent is not held accountable to her child for careless supervision.

Holodook versus Spencer, decided by the Supreme Court of Columbia County, New York, in January, 1973, decision rendered by Judge A. Franklin Mahoney.
Formal legal citation: 340 N.Y.S. (2d) 311

Taking the Law Into His Own Hands
Dean is guilty, because the shot would have caused the death by itself.

State of California versus Lewis, decided by a panel of three Judges of the Supreme Court of California, in May, 1899, decision rendered by Judge Temple.
Formal legal citation: 57 Pac. 470

Armed Robbery
Leander cannot be tried and convicted of both offenses, because both offenses require proof of the same facts. Therefore, the facts only support one conviction.

*United States versus Hearst, decided by a panel
of three Judges of the United States Court of
Appeals, Ninth Circuit, in March 1980, decision
rendered by Circuit Judge Choy.*
*Formal legal citation: 638 F. (2d) 1190
(California)*

Discount Theft?
Timothy is not guilty of theft over $200, because
the evidence of value was hearsay. Someone with
direct knowledge of the value of the suits should
have been called as a witness.
*Lee versus State of Arkansas, decided by a
panel of three Judges of the Supreme Court of
Arkansas, Division 1, in October, 1978.*
Formal legal citation: 571 S.W. (2d) 603

Intoxication Plus
Ralph cannot be convicted of causing death by
criminal negligence, because the blood alcohol
level only raises a presumption of intoxication.
Such evidence, by itself, is insufficient to prove
criminal negligence.
*State of Louisiana versus Williams, decided by a
panel of four Judges of the Supreme Court of
Louisiana, in October, 1977, decision rendered by
Justice Marcus, with Judge Dennis dissenting.*
Formal legal citation: 354 So. (2d) 152

Fool's Gold

Duncan can recover damages from Ned, because Ned's practical joke was premeditated and practised. It directly resulted in damages to Duncan's self-esteem.

Nickerson et al. versus Hodges et al., decided by a panel of three Judges of the Supreme Court of Louisiana, in February, 1920, decision rendered by Judge Dawkins, with Judges Sommerville and O'Neill dissenting.

Formal legal citation: 84 So. 37

Pen Pals

These letters are admissible in evidence, because they were not hearsay, but rather evidence of the mental state of the accused.

Sollars versus State of Nevada, decided by the Supreme Court of Nevada, in 1957.

Formal legal citation: 316 P. (2d) 917

Speedy Trial

Roxane cannot be tried again for the same offense, because the rule against double jeopardy (being tried twice) applies where there has been a violation of the speedy trial rule.

State of Indiana versus Roberts, decided by a panel of three Judges of the Court of Appeals of Indiana, in December, 1976, decision rendered by Chief Judge Robertson.

Formal legal citation: 358 N.E. (2d) 181

Rapid Fire

The witness can testify as to what Linda told him, because Linda's statement was a spontaneous utterance, made in response to a startling incident, without opportunity for reflection and fabrication.

State of North Carolina versus Johnson, decided by the Supreme Court of North Carolina, in January, 1978, decision rendered by Judge Copeland.

Formal legal citation: 239 S.E. (2d) 806

Practical Joker

Morris is guilty, because he should have foreseen the risk of injury. His behavior was a gross deviation from the standard of care that an ordinary person would have exercised.

State of Utah versus Hallett and Felsch, decided by a panel of four Judges of the Supreme Court of Utah, in October, 1980, decision rendered by Chief Justice Crockett.

Formal legal citation: 619 P. (2d) 335

Sign of the Times

Steve was not successful, because criticism of public officials in their capacity as such is sanctioned by the constitution, unless such criticism is false and motivated by actual malice. There was no proof of actual malice here and no defamation action can be taken.

New York Times Company versus Sullivan, decided by a panel of six Judges of the United States Supreme Court, in January, 1964, decision rendered by Judge Brennan.
Formal legal citation: 376. U.S. 254

The Naked Truth?
The police in no way violated Edmund's privilege against self-incrimination.

Schmerber versus State of California, decided by a panel of nine Judges of the United States Supreme Court, in April, 1966, decision rendered by Judge Brennan representing the opinions of five judges, with dissenting opinions rendered by Judges Warren, Black, Douglas, Fortas.
Formal legal citation: 384 U.S. 757

A Misfire
Alan has to pay despite the common error, because Alan got what he had asked for under the contract. His misunderstanding does not relieve him from the obligation to pay.

Upton-on-Severn Rural District Council versus Powell, decided by a panel of three Judges of the Court of Appeal, in January, 1942, decision rendered by Lord Greene.
Formal legal citation: [1942] 1 All E.R. 220 (England)

Double Dose of Cyanide

The evidence is not admissible, because no connection was shown between Henry and the first wife's poisoning.

Noor Mohamed versus The King, decided by a panel of five Judges of the Judicial Committee of the Privy Council in November, 1949, decision rendered by Lord Uthwatt.

Formal legal citation: [1949] A.C. 182 (U.K.)

The Fatal Hostage

They are guilty of murder, because the death of Caroline would not have occurred had Steve and Tim not committed the robbery.

Jackson and Wells Jr. versus the State of Maryland, decided by a panel of seven Judges of the Court of Appeals of Maryland, in December, 1979, decision rendered by Judge Orth.

Formal legal citation: 408 A. (2d) 711

Invasion of Privacy?

Val cannot recover damages because there was no "publicity" here. Only Val's relatives and employer were contacted, and such a small group does not satisfy the requirement of publicity.

*Vogel Jr. and Smith versus WT Grant Company,
decided by a panel of two Judges of the Supreme
Court of Pennsylvania, in October, 1974, decision
rendered by Judge Manderino.*
Formal legal citation: 327 A. (2d) 133

The Other Woman
Mac must testify about the "other woman,"
because he is seeking judgment in his favor.
He must therefore subject himself to cross-
examination.

*Nuckols versus Nuckols, decided by a panel of
three Judges of the District Court of Appeal of
Florida, in September, 1966, decision rendered by
Judge Lopez.*
Formal legal citation: 189 So. (2d) 832

Expensive Upgrade
Cedric can recover $100,000 from Montgomery,
because Cedric is entitled to the land at a uniform
grade, even if the cost is disproportionate to the
value of the land.

*Groves versus Wunder, decided by a panel of
two Judges of the Supreme Court of Minnesota, in
April, 1939, decision rendered by Justice Stone.*
Formal legal citation: 286 N.W. 235

Not Presumed Innocent

The statement is not sufficient to result in a mistrial. It was nothing more than an explanation to the jury of its right to find the defendant guilty.

The People of the State of Illinois versus Mathews, decided by a panel of three Judges of the Appellate Court of Illinois, Third District, in February, 1979, decision rendered by Judge Stengel.
Formal legal citation: 387 N.E. (2d) 10

Take the Money and Run

The widow cannot keep the money, because money paid under a mistake of fact can generally be recovered.

Kelly versus Solari, decided by the U.K. Court of Exchequer, in November, 1841.
Formal legal citation: 152 E.R. 24 (U.K.)

Bad Publicity

Millie should be successful in her action for defamation, because Millie was not a public figure. She did not assume any role of special prominence in the affairs of society nor did she "thrust herself to the forefront of any particular controversy in order to influence the resolution of the issues involved in it."

*Time, Inc. versus Firestone, decided by a panel
of four Judges of the United States Supreme Court,
in October, 1975, decision rendered by Judges
Powell, Brennan, White and Marshall.*

Formal legal citation: 424 U.S. 448

Twice Cruel

Natalie cannot place this in evidence. Evidence of
a party's bad character is not generally admissible.

*Bosworth versus Bosworth, decided by the
Supreme Court of Errors of Connecticut, in
November, 1944, decision rendered by Judge
Dickinson.*

Formal legal citation: 40 A. (2d) 186

The Right Charge

Eunice is not guilty of theft, because there was a
contract of sale. She was therefore guilty of fraud,
not theft.

*Regina versus Dawood, decided by a panel of
three Judges of the Alberta Supreme Court, Appellate Division, in September, 1975, decision rendered by Judge McDermid, with Judge Clement
dissenting.*

*Formal legal citation: [1976] 1 W.W.R. 262
(Canada)*

The Ends Justify the Means?

Jake's confession is admissible, because force was applied to discover the girl's location and not to extract a confession. The violence did not taint the confession.

Leon versus State of Florida, decided by a panel of Judges of the Florida Court of Appeal, Third District, in February, 1982, with Judge Ferguson dissenting.

Formal legal citation: 31 Cr. L. 2038

She Never Heard of Henry

Kate is not guilty, because her answer in no way interrupted the police's progress towards their objective.

The State of Ohio versus Stephens, decided by a panel of three Judges of the Court of Appeals of Ohio, Hamilton County, in July, 1978.

Formal legal citation: 387 N.E. (2d) 252

The Fatal Trip

Abe died by "external, violent and accidental means," within the meaning of the insurance policy, because the fall was the immediate cause of death. This fall was properly characterized as an accident.

Moran versus Massachusetts Mutual Life Insurance Co., decided by a panel of three Judges of the Supreme Court, Appellate Term, First Department, in June, 1941.
Formal legal citation: 29 N.Y.S. (2d) 33

The Belligerent Victim
The evidence is admissible, because a victim's reputation for violence is generally admissible.

Freeman versus State of Mississippi, decided by a panel of four Judges of the Supreme Court of Mississippi, in December, 1967.
Formal legal citation: 204 So. (2d) 842

Hair Today and Tomorrow
Shirley won, because the advertisement was an offer. Shirley accepted the offer. There was a contract.

Goldthorpe versus Logan, decided by a panel of three Judges of the Ontario Court of Appeal, in March, 1943, decision rendered by Judge Laidlaw.
Formal legal citation: [1943] O.W.N. 215 (Canada)

Unfaded Memory

The evidence is sufficient to convict Mario of the offense, even though the identification was made out of court. A jury could find Mario guilty beyond a reasonable doubt.

Bedford versus State of Maryland, decided by a panel of seven Judges of the Maryland Court of Appeals, in March, 1982, with three Judges dissenting.

Formal legal citation: 31 Cr. L. 2056

Mass Produced

Avery is not guilty of the offense, because the language of the law does not apply to modern commercially manufactured products, such as brand-name watches.

The People of the State of New York versus James, decided by the District Court, Nassau County, First District, Criminal Part 1, in October, 1974, decision rendered by Judge Ralph Diamond.

Formal legal citation: 361 N.Y.S. (2d) 255

Blood Rights

The judge can authorize the transfusion, because the state has an interest in the conservation of life. The hospital authorities should be allowed to exercise medical judgment in the face of the parents' refusal.

John F. Kennedy Memorial Hospital versus Heston and Heston, decided by a panel of six Judges of the Supreme Court of New Jersey, in February, 1971, decision rendered by Judge Weintraub.
Formal legal citation: 279 A. (2d) 670

Stabbed and Twice Dropped

Mildred is guilty, because the stab wound was a contributing factor in the death.

R. versus Smith, decided by the Courts-Martial Appeal Court, in March, 1959, decision rendered by The Lord Chief Justice, Mr. Justice Streatfield.
Formal legal citation: 43 Cr. App. R. 121 (England)

Unwarranted Measures?

Morton is found guilty, because the police didn't rely on the arrest warrant to make the arrest. The ruse did not violate the accused's constitutional rights.

State of Washington versus Myers, decided by the Washington Court of Appeals, in August, 1983.
Formal legal citation: 33 Cr. L. 2505

Convenience Store Mugging

Alice is successful, because it is the store owner's duty to his customers to take reasonable care in providing a safe place at which to shop.

Butler versus Acme Markets Inc., decided by the New Jersey Supreme Court, in May, 1982.

Formal legal citation: 31 Cr. L. 2222

Murder, She Said

Abigail is guilty of conspiring to commit murder, because her trip and discussions with the police officer were an overt act made in furtherance of the plan to kill her rival.

Blaylock versus the State of Oklahoma, decided by a panel of three Judges of the Court of Criminal Appeals of Oklahoma, in July, 1979, decision rendered by Judge Bussey.

Formal legal citation: 598 P. (2d) 251

Home Cooking

The prosecution can place in evidence the deaths of the two sons, because Cynthia prepared the food and she alone did not suffer from arsenic poisoning.

Regina versus Geering, decided by a panel of three Judges of a U.K. Court, in August, 1849.

Formal legal citation: 18 L.J. MC. 215 (UK.)

The Case of the Slippery Floor

The defense may show this, because the evidence was so extensive as to justify an inference of a history of safety.

Erickson versus Walgreen Drug Co. et al., decided by a panel of three Judges of the Supreme Court of Utah, in June, 1951, decision rendered by Judge Wolfe.

Formal legal citation: 232 P. (2d) 210

The Tired Lawyer

Rose's appeal should be allowed, because a sleeping lawyer is the same as no lawyer at all. Actual prejudice need not be shown.

Javor versus United States, decided by a panel of Judges of the United States Court of Appeals for the Ninth Circuit, in January, 1984, with Judge Anderson dissenting.

Formal legal citation: 34 Cr. L. 2375

You Can Rely on Us

The bank succeeds, because accountants are liable to any person who might reasonably be expected to rely on their statements.

Haig versus Bamford, decided by a panel of nine Judges of the Supreme Court of Canada, in April, 1976.

Formal legal citation: [1977] 1 S.C.R. 466 (Canada)

Cruise Control

Pierre is guilty of speeding, because by delegating partial control of his car through the use of the speed control, Pierre was the agent who caused the act of speeding.

State of Kansas versus Baker, decided by a panel of three Judges of the Court of Appeals of Kansas, in August, 1977, decision rendered by Judge Spencer.

Formal legal citation: 571 P. (2d) 65

Tennis, Anyone?

Renee should be allowed to play, because the chromosome test is unfair, discriminatory and inequitable; it concentrates on only one factor in ascertaining sex and does not allow consideration of other factors.

Richards versus United States Tennis Association, U.S. Open Tennis Championship Committee and Women's Tennis Association, Inc., decided by the Supreme Court, Special Term, New York County, Part 1, in August, 1977, decision rendered by Judge Alfred Ascione.

Formal legal citation: 400 N.Y.S. 2d 267

Buying Votes?

The court ordered a mistrial, because it is improper to allow a jury and a party to a trial to fraternize.

Scott versus Tubbs, decided by a panel of three Judges of the Supreme Court of Colorado, in April, 1908, decision rendered by Judge Steele.
Formal legal citation: 95 P. 540

Leader of the Pact

Alex is not guilty, because this was really a double attempted suicide. At most he would be guilty of aiding and abetting a suicide.

Forden versus Joseph G., decided by the California Supreme Court, in August, 1983.
Formal legal citation: 33 Cr. L. 2511

Policing the Police

The Police Department is guilty of negligence, because it was reasonably foreseeable that an officer unfit to carry a gun might injure members of his family.

Bonsignore versus City of New York, decided by the United States Court of Appeals for the Second Circuit, in June, 1982.
Formal legal citation: 31 Cr. L. 2294

Illegal Search?

The evidence is admissible, because searches of open fields do not violate any reasonable expectation of privacy.

United States of America versus Oliver, decided by a panel of five Judges of the United States Court of Appeals, Sixth Circuit, in February, 1982, decision rendered by Judge Bailey Brown, and Judges Keith, Edwards Jr., Lively and Jones dissenting.
Formal legal citation: 686 F. (2d) 356

Cost Cutting

The law is invalid, because it arbitrarily discriminates against the most seriously injured victims of medical malpractice.

Wright versus Central Du Page Hospital Association, decided by a panel of three Judges of the Supreme Court of Illinois, in May, 1976, decision rendered by Judge Goldenhersh and Judges Underwood and Ryan partially dissenting.
Formal legal citation: 347 N.E. (2d) 736

Shocking Pictures

The pictures are admissible, because direct evidence of injuries is generally admissible, notwithstanding its effect upon the jury.

People of the State of California versus Kemp, decided by a panel of Judges of the Supreme Court of California, in January, 1974, with Judge McComb dissenting.
Formal legal citation: 517 P. (2d) 826

Child Neglect?

Isabel is not guilty of child neglect, because there was no recognized or recognizable dangerous condition in Isabel's house from which substantial and unjustifiable risk could be inferred.

State of Oregon versus Goff, decided by a panel of Judges of the Oregon Court of Appeals, in January, 1984, with three Judges dissenting.

Formal legal citation: 34 Cr. L. 2409

Less Than Meets the Eye

Jim is not guilty of robbery in the first degree, because the language of the law leads to the inescapable conclusion that actual possession of a weapon is a requirement for a conviction.

State of New Jersey versus Butler, decided by a panel of Judges of the New Jersey Supreme Court, in May, 1982, with two Judges dissenting.

Formal legal citation: 31 Cr. L. 2220

Once or Forever?

Daniel is not guilty, because the crime was committed when Daniel accepted the coat. Mere possession of the coat was not a continuing crime.

Duncan versus the State of Maryland, decided by a panel of two Judges of the Court of Appeals of Maryland, in April, 1978, decision rendered by Judge Orth and concurring decision rendered by Chief Judge Murphy.
Formal legal citation: 384 A. (2d) 456

A Matter of Faith

Igor should be admitted to the university, because it did not require vaccination of Christian Scientists. To exclude Igor would be to show preference for one set of religious beliefs over another.

Kolbeck versus Kramer and Rutgers, The State University, decided by a panel of seven Judges of the Supreme Court of New Jersey, in October, 1965.
Formal legal citation: 214 A. (2d) 408

Serendipity in the Third

The evidence is admissible, because evidence can be admitted to show that the establishment was a bookie joint. It would violate the hearsay rule only if it were admitted to show that the *State of Connecticut versus Tolisano, decided by a panel of five Judges of the Supreme Court of Errors of Connecticut, in November, 1949, decision rendered by Judge Jennings.*
Formal legal citation: 70 A. (2d) 118

Ambulance-Chasing

Fabian is not guilty, because the statute is too broad; for example, it might prohibit a friend who was a lawyer from advising an injured victim.

People of the State of Michigan versus Posner, decided by the Court of Appeals of Michigan, in October, 1977, decision rendered by Judge Kaufman.

Formal legal citation: 261 N.W. (2d) 209

Unfinished Business

They are not guilty, because there was no actual entry into the store. The most they could have been convicted of was an attempt to break and enter.

Stamps versus Commonwealth of Kentucky, decided by a panel of six Judges of the Supreme Court of Kentucky, in July, 1980.

Formal legal citation: 602 S.W. (2d) 172

On-the-Job Training

Lloyd's appeal is not successful, because actual errors in handling the case must be demonstrated before reversal will be granted.

United States of America versus Cronic, decided by a panel of two Judges of the United States Supreme Court, in January, 1984, decision rendered by Judge Stevens.

Formal legal citation: 104 Sct. 2039

The Good News and the Bad News

Utility cannot recover from Dr. Smith's insurer, because Utility's claim against Dr. Smith, whom it employed, was not for malpractice but rather for breach of contract or fraud.

McFarling versus Azar, decided by a panel of three Judges of the United States Court of Appeal, Fifth Circuit, in September, 1975, decision rendered by Judge Golbold.

Formal legal citation: 519 F. (2d) 1075 (Fla)

RULES OF THE GAME

With two or more, you can turn "What's the Verdict: Test your Legal Knowledge" into a game. The rules are simple:

Player # 1 reads the facts of a case and tries to figure out the trial court decision. If it is correct, Player #1 gets one point. The other players are free to appeal that decision.

A price must be paid, however, for the right to appeal: three points. (In this game, as in real life, justice is not cheap.)

If the appealing player or players are unsuccessful, they simply lose the three points. If they are successful, however, each receives four points and Player #1 loses two points.

If Player #1 is incorrect in predicting the trial decision, he loses one point. Only he has the right to appeal that finding. He too must pay three points in order to exercise his right of appeal.

If he is incorrect on appeal, he will have lost four points total. If he is successful on appeal, he wins five points. In other words, a player who is wrong at trial but who wins on appeal gains one point in the process.

To summarize, here are the possible results for Player #1 after a case has been completed:

- a gain of one point if he correctly predicts the trial outcome and is not challenged—or if he is challenged and the decision is upheld on appeal.

- a loss of one point if he correctly predicts the trial outcome but the trial decision is reversed on appeal.
- a loss of one point if he incorrectly predicts the trial outcome and chooses not to appeal.
- a loss of four points if he incorrectly predicts the trial outcome and unsuccessfully appeals.

The following are the possible results for a player who chooses to appeal a correct finding by Player #1:

- a gain of one point if the appeal is successful.
- a loss of three points if the appeal is unsuccessful.

The players take turns reading the cases. The game ends when one player reaches ten points. Scores can go negative, and don't be surprised if this happens quite often, until players recognize the true cost of litigation.

INDEX